NOT AFRAID

SECRETS OF EMINEM

LISA GARDINER

Not Afraid: Secrets of Eminem by Lisa Gardiner
© 2019 Lisa Gardiner

CHAPTER ONE

"By the way, if you see my dad. Tell him that I slit his throat in this dream I had."

"So yeah dad let's walk
Let's have us a father and son talk
But I bet we probably wouldn't get one block
Without me knocking your block off"

———

Beginnings
(I Actually Learned a Lot from You.
You Taught Me What Not to Do.)

PICTURE A LITTLE BOY OF SEVEN OR EIGHT SITTING ON THE worn, tan carpet of a trailer, or cheap rental. Just sitting on the floor, using his red and black crayons to color in his Spiderman coloring book. The phone rings, and his auntie Edna gets up from the chintz couch.

On the phone is her brother Marshall Bruce Mathers II, otherwise known as "Bruce".

When the little boy hears the name "Bruce," he begins to feel a bit light-headed, his stomach clenches, his heart beats painfully fast.

Maybe his dad has finally read one of his letters? Maybe Bruce will finally, swoop back into his life, and stop the bullies who bash him and make him cry from pain at least once a week.

Or perhaps his father will come to pick him up, take him to live in a nice area, with a good school. A school where he won't be bashed and stolen from anymore. They took his shoes and his lunch money last week and splashed him with orange juice wetting his *Star Wars* t-shirt. They stole his *Mork and Mindy* book that Aunt Edna gave him for Christmas, and wouldn't give it back.

And maybe if he could live with his dad sometimes, he wouldn't have to deal with mom's mood swings quite so often either. That would cool!

But even if he can't live with his dad, it would still be great to talk to him on the phone. Bruce might give him some fatherly advice. Like dads on *Happy Days* or *The Brady Bunch,* dads giving pep talks to their sons, dads sharing wisdom and knowledge. That's what he needs. Advice for getting on better with mom, handling bullies, making new friends.

As Edna talks to her brother, the child's hope and excitement build in tandem with his dread.

Will his dad finally ask to speak to him? Has Bruce read all the letters he sent? He did a pretty cool drawing of *Aqua Man,* fighting *Captain Demo* on the last letter he sent to his dad. He was proud of that one. He wrote a poem about *Aqua Man* too. Maybe Bruce will be impressed enough by his last letter to talk to him. His drawings and poems are gifts for his dad.

Aunt Edna said his dad is a really good guy (not bad like Mom says) He works in hotels. Marshall knows that when he grows up, he's going to be a comic book artist and make his own comics. Marshall Mathers will create the greatest superhero ever! And have comics in all the papers and his own comic books. His superhero will even have a movie!

But…. no. So far, all of the letters come back marked *"Return to Sender. No such person."* Maybe he messed up writing the addresses. Next letter he'll be super careful with his handwriting. But today will dad talk to him? He's right here, coloring on the floor and his dad's on the phone with Aunt Edna. He *has* to ask to speak to him this time.

IT NEVER HAPPENS. Bruce *never* once asks to speak to his own son Marshall. The letters all come back, even though his father's own sister Edna gave little Marshall the correct address to send.

Next time he "writes the addresses on 'em perfect". But there's still no reply.

Horrifyingly, Debbie has admitted that she recognized Bruce's handwriting. She claims that she is sure it was her ex-husband Bruce who wrote *"Return to Sender. No such person here."* on all the envelopes containing his little son's letters and drawings, in one of the most callous rejections of a little child imaginable.

Sarah Mathers (Eminem's half-sister) has said that she can remember watching Bruce write *Return to Sender* on the envelope, and then sticking the unopened letter back in the post.

Although Eminem himself has never spelled it out publicly, it seems clear that he eventually realized his father was the one writing *Return to Sender* on all the envelopes, containing all his heartfelt childish letters and drawings. His total rejection of his father's efforts to contact him once he became famous seems to indicate that he believes his mom on this one.

When asked on camera by the media if he would ever want to meet and reconcile with his dad, Marshall pauses, smiles, and says in a very polite but slightly sinister voice, "No. I don't think so." The smile and the polite voice somehow have a cutting, savage edge. The smile and sound of pure revenge.

―――――

MARSHALL BRUCE MATHERS III was born on October 17, 1972, in St. Joseph, Missouri. His mother reportedly had excruciating seventy-two-hour labor.

Oddly the father who later wanted nothing to do with Marshall, named him after himself, without even consulting Debbie at all.

While she was in a coma, Bruce told staff the baby's name was Marshall Bruce Mathers III.

Debbie has said she did mind this because she loved her father in law Marshall Bruce Mathers Snr., who was always very kind to her.

Perhaps this is a mark of a true narcissist, giving a baby your own exact name but then completely abandoning the child six months later?

One can only speculate on reasons why Bruce treated little Marshall the horrible way he did.

The first possibility is that Bruce believed that acknowledging his little son, in any way, would trigger child support claims. The other possibility is that Bruce hated Debbie Mathers so much that he wanted to reject the child he had made with her.

It is possible Debbie was too scared to make child support claims. She alleges Bruce beat her repeatedly and severely. Eminem mentions the missing child support in the song *My Mom*.

> *Child support, your father, he ain't sent the shit*
> *And so, what if he did? It's none of your dang*
>   *business, kid*

Bruce went on to have two more children with his new wife, their names being Michael and Sarah. Eminem briefly mentions them in the song *Marshall Mathers*.

> *All of a sudden, I got ninety-some cousins (Hey,*
>   *it's me!)*
> *A half-brother and sister who never seen me*
> *Or even bothered to call me, until they saw me on TV*

Eminem has three (known) half-siblings. But Michael and Sarah, his father's children, were never people he knew at all growing up.

There are rumors that Marshall rejected Sarah multiple times as she tried to meet him at concerts, even refusing one time to get out of the tour bus, while she was right outside. But there are also rumors that he eventually met up with her alone at least one time.

The names Mathers, Michael, and Sarah are all common names, and many bloggers and journalists have posted pictures of various attractive "Sarah Mathers" that are probably *not* Eminem's sister. One of these women is a dancer named Sarah Mathers, that is clearly way too young to be Marshall's sister. People on YouTube keep asking the dancer if she's Eminem's sister. She never replies, possibly in order to use the mystery for her career. Or maybe she doesn't respond because she fears drama.

If you google "Sarah Mathers" a few different pictures come up on blogs with the bloggers claiming these women are Eminem's sister. None of them are. They are just clickbait. There are many poorly written articles online spreading misinformation about various aspects of Eminem's life for clickbait.

The only picture of Sarah online (as of 2019) that actually appears to be Marshall's real half-sister comes from a Cosmo (or similar) magazine article "I'm Eminem's Secret Sister," in which Sarah describes her heartbreak because she's been unable to meet up with Marshall.

Marshall's little half-brother Nathan (his mother's child whose father is Frank Samara) is the only sibling Eminem considers his "real" brother.

Nathan was born when Marshall was fourteen years old. Eminem has claimed he raised Nathan, and as soon as he could afford to, he adopted him.

According to Debbie, though, Eminem may have even more half brothers and sisters. Once Eminem fame reached the heights of his second album, Debbie suddenly got a phone call from Bruce, who was all of a sudden desperate to get in touch with Marshall.

Bruce started the conversation by telling Debbie he "vaguely" recalled their marriage. Then he told her that he'd heard that Heather, a young woman he had cheated on her with while married, had had children by him.

Bruce also told Debbie there were rumors that he had

several other children. Debbie asked him how many children he had, and Bruce said: "I don't know." Debbie said, "you're a piece of work" and hung up the phone.

A former security guard tells of how one time at a concert in Missouri, Eminem was confronted by a group of teenagers, waving birth certificates claiming to be related to him on his father's side.

Marshall ignored them, and security asked them to leave. This occurred as Marshall hit a new level of fame, with staggering sales, and with all the pressure he was under, it's hard to blame him for giving these kids the cold shoulder.

Eminem's father is quoted in interviews, as saying it was his son Michael, who first told him that there was a new rapper on the scene with the same name as he had, just after *My Name Is* became a hit.

Marshall's first song to appear on TV as a music video was *Just Don't Give (Just Don't Give a Fuck* on the uncensored version.*)* This song did not make the charts in any country.

However, Marshall's second song *My Name Is* was Eminem's first truly big hit, peaking at number 2, on the UK charts, and 4 in Ireland and New Zealand, but only reaching 36 on the US charts

But even after the relative success of *The Slim Shady LP* and the hit single *My Name Is,* Marshall's father *still* never tried to contact him.

During that period, Eminem told the press that he was glad his father had not tried to reach out to him because if he saw him, he'd beat the crap out of him.

Later, however, at the absolute height of Eminem's fame, after his second major studio album, and the massive worldwide success of the songs *Stan, The Way I Am,* and *The Real Slim Shady.* Eminem's "father" would finally make a desperate and pathetic attempt to reconnect with his multi-millionaire son. Bruce took out a full-page ad in *News of the World*

He wrote an open letter to his son, which was published in the *Daily Mirror* in 2001. (Bruce only paid for such a letter after Marshall's performance of Stan with Elton John at the Grammys.) The open letter began:

"Hello, son. You won't remember me, though I held you in my arms when you were a baby.

You think I dumped you and your mother and never came looking for you. You're convinced I'm a drunk who never answered any of your letters. Well, I want you to read this and realize you've been fed lies all your life. Now you'll hear the truth for the first time."

In this letter, Bruce goes on to claims that he didn't leave his baby, that it was Debbie who packed up and left him taking all the furniture and belongings without a word, leaving no details of where his son was. Bruce claimed that because he had to work at his job and earn a living, he didn't have time to track them down.

While Eminem steadfastly ignored this letter, he did finally kind of answer it, twelve years later, in the lyrics to his song *Headlights*.

One thing I never asked was
Where the fuck my deadbeat dad was
Fuck it, I guess he had trouble keepin' up with every
*   address*

*But I'd a flipped every mattress, every rock, and desert
    cactus
Owned a collection of maps
And followed my kids to the edge of the atlas
Someone ever moved them from me? That you could
    bet your asses
If I had to come down the chimney dressed as Santa,
    kidnap them*

Eminem didn't agree that having to hold down a job was a reason to give up looking for a baby boy.

Bruce also claimed in his "open letter" that his sister Edna told him that Debbie asked her not to tell him where baby Marshall or his brother were living.

But Debbie tells a very different story. She claims that sometimes, when Bruce came home drunk, he would scream, "Cook me a meal, bitch!" Then when she presented him with the meal, he would throw it on the floor and kick her while she cleaned it up.

She alleges that Bruce would often throw baby "Micky" into his playpen, shouting, "The fucking little brat can wait" before beating on his wife. At this stage of his life baby, Marshall was called Mick and Micky after Micky Mouse because of his exceptionally large ears.

On his album *Revival,* Eminem sings about baby Hailie

*"You got your momma's personality, same eyes as
    I got
Her beautiful smile, but your ears are the same size as
    mine are
Sorry for that, (laughs) a little minor mishap
But you'll grow into 'em, baby."*

Indeed, both Hailie and Marshall "grew into them," so that their large ears never looked out of place on their adult selves. Debbie's problems with Bruce did not end with being kicked while cleaning up the mess he made. According to Debbie's heart-breaking recollection, baby, Micky would often touch her black eyes and say "boo boo?"

His mother alleged that her final straw was the time Bruce smashed her face into a neighbor's door over and over again in a drunken rage, shattering her nose and leaving blood everywhere.

Unlike Bruce's claims, however, Debbie says she took almost nothing with her, not the car she owned that was in her name, not the money lying in envelopes in the house for paying electricity, not Marshall's baby book which indeed turned up later in a German magazine interview with Bruce showed it off, catching him out in the lie that Debbie left "taking everything."

While Debbie can be seen as something of an unreliable narrator in her 2008 memoir, *My Son Marshall, My Son Eminem*, the same might be said of Eminem. The truth surely lies somewhere in between. But on the subject of Eminem's father, the two are pretty much in agreement.

Bruce actually did contact Marshall one time. Eminem was sixteen, and Debbie phoned him one day. Kim had been searching for her father inspiring Marshall to reach out to Debbie and ask her to do the same. Bruce agreed to send a letter.

But when the one page letter came with a picture of Bruce holding a surfboard and suggesting Marshall make a quick trip to California to ride the waves with him, Eminem was not impressed.

After a fatherless childhood of school beatings and poverty, the two-paragraph letter infuriated the late teen.

Marshall chose to ignore it, beginning an adult lifetime of treating his father the way Bruce had treated his son.

The story of Bruce Mathers is almost comical in what a cautionary tale it is for deadbeat dads everywhere. The child you abandoned for fear of being hit for child support might become a multi-millionaire.

A very similar story occurred, with the infamous Dr. Phil guest, the "cash me outside" girl, and new school hip-hop "performance artist" Danielle Bregoli, who goes by the stage name of Bhad Bhabie.

While obviously a vastly less successful celebrity than Eminem, Bregoli at sixteen already has a reported net worth of four million and rapidly climbing much to the disgust of some hip-hop fans who disapprove of the way she was "discovered" and of the fact she has ghost writers.

Bregoli's father (who allegedly relinquished his rights to care for her when she was two, in exchange for not paying child support) came out of the woodwork when her net worth reached 2 million to suddenly say he really wanted to be in her life.

Both fathers blame their kids' mothers for the estrangement from their offspring and the years of silence. But neither celebrity buys their excuses.

Danielle Bregoli is the kind of new up and coming "hip hop star" that Eminem rails against on his 2019 album *Kamikaze* in his song *Lucky You,* among others.

I got a couple of mansions
Still, I don't have any manners
You got a couple of ghostwriters
But to these kids, it don't actually matter
They're askin' me, "What the fuck happened to hip-
hop?"

I said, "I don't have any answers."

She is the epitome of the up and comers that disgust Eminem, chosen for her looks, and using trap beats she didn't write, but admittedly, she has great flow.

The comparisons between the two stars came to a head with fans of Bhad Bhabie claiming the beat for *Not Alike* was too similar to Bregoli's hit *Hi Bitch*. Many Eminem fans prefer to think Eminem was parodying the rapper Migos and his song *Bad and Boujee*.

But *Not Alike* and *Hi Bitch* were both produced by Ronald Oneil Spence, Jr. known professionally as Ronny J, so this could account for their similar sound.

Surprisingly, Ronny J also produced Machine Gun Kelly's *Rap Devil*.

There is no question that *Not Alike* uses a trap beat, and that Eminem is mocking the new style rappers such as Migos, Bregoli and Lil Pump in the song by naming random things, that have no seeming correlation to each other.

However, Marshall still can't resist being wittier than these rappers artfully connecting things, like eyes drops to Cyclops (the one-eyed monster) in his seemingly aimless start to the song. By starting the song with the word "brain dead," Marshall also makes another diss.

Braindead, eye drops
Pain meds, cyclops
Daybed, iPod
"May-back", Maybach
Train wrecks, sidewalks
Payless, high-tops
K-Fed, iHop
Playtex, icebox

"May-back, Maybach," appears to be a direct hit at Bregoli who pronounces the car's name wrong that way, and also appeared in a video rapping about her Maybach when the car in her video was not even a Maybach.

Some hardcore Eminem fans seem offended by the very idea that Eminem would even know of Bregoli's existence. However, in the 2018 song *Killshot*, Eminem even references Lil Tay a nine-year-old who while basing her "act" on rich hip-hop stars, never even attempted to rap a single bar.

This little girl was only briefly infamous, because her sixteen-year-old brother, wrote bizarre performance pieces for her to put up on *YouTube*.

Lil Tay's schtick was to pretend to be an extremely bratty, extremely wealthy kid, parodying some famous rappers' "flexing" or bragging.

In these videos Lil' Tay did nothing but kick expensive cars, throw fifty-dollar bills and designer handbags around and scream about her wealth. She often used hip-hop type phrases.

Eminem keeps abreast of all pop culture phenomena in case he can work it into a line. And he proved that by dropping the name of Lil' Tay. As a diss to MGK, who is 18 years younger many listeners found it hilarious.

In his Kamikaze song *Lucky You* with Joyner Lucas, Eminem complains about the Bregoli kind of "hip hop" stars even more.

But nothin' is feeling like anyone has any fuckin'
    ability
To even stick to a subject, it's killin' me
The inability to pen humility
Ha-ta-ta ba-ta-ta, why don't we make a bunch of
Fuckin' songs about nothin' and mumble 'em?

Regardless, there is no question that Mathers and Bregoli allegedly have similar dead-beat dads, and both are a cautionary tale for those who would abandon their children.

Bregoli made sure her mother won custody of her and even asked a judge to let her remove Peskowitz's name from her birth certificate. Her requests were granted.

Although Eminem's father told the *Star*, "I desperately want to meet him and tell him I love him. I'm not interested in his money.

The *San Diego Reader* made fun of Bruce saying that he certainly wanted money to *discuss* his famous son. When the *San Diego Reader* offered $50 for his story, Bruce scoffed and told them that "Nicole from *The Sun*" had offered him a lot more.

At this point, Bruce was a factory worker in Chula Vista, California. His then girlfriend Teresa Harbin reported that *The Star* had allegedly promised Bruce money for his interview but never followed through and had photographed him outside an AA meeting.

Bruce then claimed he'd been at the nearby *Dunkin Donuts*, not the AA. Meeting. He was reportedly quite upset by *The Star*.

Sadly, on 26 June 2019, Marshall Bruce Mathers Jr. died of a heart attack in Fort Wayne, Indiana, at the age of sixty-seven having never in his life had a conversation with his famous son.

Marshall had his mom, and the two were close during his childhood. But he resented that she dropped him off with his Aunt Edna, for months at a time, while she worked as a cab driver to support him.

As well as her career as a cab driver, Debbie Mathers also sporadically worked as a door to door Avon saleslady, including while heavily pregnant with Nathan.

Unfortunately, Debbie had to quit her jobs after he was beaten so severely by D'Angelo Baily that he ended up in the hospital, and she had to help him recover. Then she ended up in a car accident that led to chronic pain and attempts to dull that pain with prescription drugs.

The fact that Debbie never worked after Eminem turned nine led to his accusations that his mom "never ever worked."

Addiction to prescription drugs crept up on Debbie as it has for many famous Americans, such as Michael Jackson, and as it later would for her own son.

Eminem's humble beginnings, growing up with a single drug-addicted mom, and having a dad who never paid a penny of child support seem to have affected his political leanings. Marshall has written some powerful political songs.

His political leanings have even led to run-ins with both Presidents Bush and Trump, and even to three separate visits from the Secret Service, who investigated him as a potential threat to the USA, and to the life of the president on three separate occasions.

CHAPTER TWO

Run the faucet, I'ma dunk
A bunch of Trump supporters underwater
Snuck up on 'em in Ray-Bans in a gray van with a
   spray tan

———

Politics
(*Fork and Dagger*)

IN 2004, ALONGSIDE THAT YEAR'S US PRESIDENTIAL election, MTV put on a special "convention" called *The Shady National Convention*. This was MTV's mock campaign to celebrate the debut of *Shade 45*, Eminem's Sirius XM radio channel.

The Shady National Convention was a concert disguised as a political convention with cabinet members 50 Cent and Dr. Dre, campaign manager Ludacris, and an endorsement from "unofficial NYC mayor" P. Diddy.

Famous businessman Donald Trump, who at the time was

a Democrat, like most of his New York friends, was invited to the Convention to introduce Slim Shady to the fans.

Here is the full text of what Trump said:

> *"Nice group, nice group. Okay, listen, listen, listen. When the Shady Party called me and told me there's going to be a convention, I said, 'it's gotta be a really big one, and it's gotta be right here in New York. Because this is the best city anywhere in the world!' Am I right? Of course, I'm right! I'm always right!*
>
> *I'm Donald Trump, I'm always right! I know a winner when I see one. And Donald Trump is telling you right now; Slim Shady is a winner! He's got brains, he's got guts, and he's got Donald Trump's vote. Ladies and gentlemen, our great candidate, Slim Shady!"*

Since then, Eminem has had this to say regarding the moment.

Take it back to the Shady National Convention
Wish I woulda spit on it before I went to shake his hand
At the event, or maybe had the wherewithal
To know that he was gonna try to tear apart
Our sacred land we cherish and stand for

Eminem has said his first thought concerning Trump as a US president was, "Hey, he's a businessman, maybe Trump would be good for the economy."

But he explained further in a *Vulture* interview, "I

thought, 'we've tried everything else, why not him?' But then — and I was watching it live — he had that speech where he said Mexico is sending us rapists and criminals. I got this feeling of 'what the fuck?' From that point on, I knew it was going to be bad with him. What he's doing putting people against each other is scary fucking shit."

While Eminem's performance of *The Storm* at the *2017 Black Entertainment Television (BET) Awards*, apparently shocked many people, Eminem involving himself in politics is not new at all. He has been involved with politics both on purpose and inadvertently since the release of his third album, *The Eminem Show*.

Horrifyingly and ironically, Eminem's song *White America* from his 2002 album *The Eminem Show* was used as a torture method in the Iraqi War in the 2000s.

US interrogators seeking to disorientate, and break Iraqi prisoners would play *White America* for days on end at the loudest possible volumes. While this practice was conveyed to the public as "torture-lite." and may seem funny, playing the same piece of music for days on end at ear-splitting volumes is no joke.

Survivors say the torture method drove them to distraction, and that they have never recovered, remaining unable to listen to any music. *Kim* and *The Real Slim Shady* were also used for this heinous purpose.

The use of the song *White America* seems particularly thoughtless and ironic. The song contains lyrics like

> *Sent to lead the march right up to the steps of*
>   *Congress*
> *And piss on the lawns of the White House*
> *To burn the casket and replace it with a parental*
>   *advisory sticker*

> *To spit liquor in the faces of this democracy of*
>   *hypocrisy*
> *Fuck you, Ms. Cheney*
> *Fuck you, Tipper Gore*
> *Fuck you with the free-ness of speech this*
> *Divided States of Embarrassment will allow me*
>   *to have*
> *Fuck you!*
> *I'm just playin' America, you know I love you*

Music torture has, however, been common practice for the CIA ever since it began its "enhanced interrogation program" in the early 2000s, which coincided with Eminem's rise to fame, causing his music to hit the "torture playlist."

One Saudi captive, interrogated in a dark prison in Afghanistan, said he was subjected to *The Real Slim Shady* for 20 days. Every second, minute, hour, of each and every one of 20 days, he was listening to *The Real Slim Shady* at top volumes.

The United Nations had previously banned the use of loud music in interrogations. Yet US military personnel were ordered to keep prisoners awake by blasting ear-splittingly loud music at them — for days, weeks, or even months on end — at prisons in Iraq, Afghanistan, and Guantánamo Bay.

British citizen, Ruhal Ahmed, spent two years in Guantanamo Bay. He was never charged with any crime and was only nineteen when he was traumatized by being short-shackled to the floor in a crouching position and forced to listen to Eminem's *Kim* for hours on end at very high volume. Strobe lights were shone in his eyes.

Reflecting on the practice of music torture, Ruhal told *HuffPost* "it's worse than physical pain because you can't block it out, and you feel that you are losing your mind."

Eminem has not just inadvertently been involved in politics however.

While Eminem's first two albums focused on his personal life, his former poverty, and new fame, *The Eminem Show* contained some of his first political comments in songs.

In his 2002 song Square Dance, he raps

'Til you fuck around, get an Anthrax napkin
Inside a package, wrapped in Saran Wrap wrappin'
Open the plastic, and then you stand back, gaspin'
Fuckin' assassins hi-jackin' Amtraks, crashin'
All this terror, America demands action
Next thing you know, you've got Uncle Sam's ass askin'
To join the army or what you'll do for their Navy
You just a baby gettin' recruited at 18
You're on a plane now, eatin' their food and their baked beans
I'm 28, they gon' take you 'fore they take me

Seemingly warning his young fans that because of 9/11, there might be a draft.

When it comes to Eminem and politics, the general public seems focused on the diss track Marshall unleashed at the 2017 *BET Awards*.

And yet the freestyle *The Storm* was not even as strongly worded, or as in-depth, as the lesser-known anti-Trump track *Like Home* that appeared on Eminem's least successful album, *Revival*.

Possibly this is because Eminem ended *The Storm* with a strong declaration: *"I'm drawing in the sand a line, you're either for or against/ And if you can't decide who you like more and you're split/ On who you should stand beside, I'll do it for you with this: Fuck you! The rest of America, stand up!*

However, in his opening track to his 2018 10th studio album *Kamikaze* "*The Ringer*," Eminem reflects on the cypher, asking, "Was it even worth it?" because, in fact, he "watched his fan base shrink to thirds."

Eminem's sales of his eighth studio album *The Marshall Mathers LP 2* to date had sold one third more than his sales of his ninth studio album *Revival* that was released the same year as *The Storm*. However, sales of his 2018 tenth studio album *Kamikaze,* a surprise album that was not advertised at all (except on Twitter), were much better.

One has to wonder here, is that really ALL because of people's support for Trump? Or is it coming from support for the alt-right around the world that sees Trump as their symbol? Was this possibly Blowback from Russian propaganda? Or did Eminem temporarily lose a lot of fans who hate politics or are fed up with politics in general? Or is it really, as many claim, that Revival was not well produced?

In the 1980s, when Eminem was a teen, political songs were very popular. Now there appears to be little interest in them, or people claim they are corny. Did his interest in politics come across as outdated? As too '80s? Or was *Revival* really a "bad" album as so many claim?

The album is full of witty lines, sophisticated layers and upbeat hooks, but the audience appeared bored with the pop/rock hooks that were so popular on his seventh studio album, *Recovery*.

Eminem had expected that working with Beyoncé would be a real coup for him, especially after the tremendous popularity of his work with Rihanna.

But even working with Beyoncé did not impress some people, and the lyrically clever *Walk on Water* was panned by some, because of its old-fashioned gospel-influenced hook.

While the hook made brilliant metaphorical sense with the lyrics, many people didn't seem to get it, and just didn't like the old-timey sound.

Others made fun of the vulnerability Marhsall revealed in the song. The lyrics to *Walk on Water* express how criticism of his work has hurt him in the past. Such vulnerability was guaranteed to bring out trolls and haters. And maybe Eminem should have realized this before releasing the album *Revival*.

But Marshall was shocked when former friends, men whose careers Eminem had helped, also turned around and trashed *Revival*. Such behavior might have reminded him of an old lyric from the Slim Shady LP.

> *I'm tired of backstabbin'-ass snakes with friendly grins.*

Tyler, the Creator of *Odd Future,* tweeted, "Dear God, this song is horrible sheesh how the fuck? Earl Sweatshirt from *Odd Future* had also criticized Eminem back, saying, "If you still follow Eminem, you drink way too much Mountain Dew."

Eminem, in response, has said, "I was like… really? What the fuck?" Eminem said. "You guys were just on tour with us, and we hung out, we kicked it, made jokes."

Eminem had given *Odd Future* the privilege of opening for his shows, surely a career-boosting opportunity, and yet the members of the group did not hesitate to publicly express contempt for Eminem's latest efforts following the 2014 tour.

Even after *Odd Future* went on tour with Eminem, Tyler had also made fun of Eminem's release the same year *Shady*

XV telling *Spin* magazine, "Dude 'ShadyXV' is fucking ASS! Hahaha, why won't someone who loves him tell him NO?"

These insults led to Marshall infamously using a homophobic slur to refer to Tyler, the Creator on the *Kamikaze* song *Fall*. Eminem mentioned the fact that Tyler had used the slur to refer to himself. But he has since regretted doing so.

"I think the word that I called him on that song was one of the things where I felt like this might be too far," Eminem said in an interview with Sway.

"Because in my quest to hurt him, I realize that I was hurting a lot of other people by saying it…It was one of the things that I kept going back to and going 'I don't feel right with this.'"

This is the first time Eminem has apologized for using the word faggot. In earlier interviews Marshall claimed he only used the word because it was a word routinely thrown around by other males all his life and that it only meant "jerk" to him, that he never meant it as a homophobic slur, but in 2018 dealing with hurt fans, Marshall finally regretted it and apologized for aiming the slur at a specific gay person.

Making matters more complicated, though, was the fact that Tyler, the Creator, before he came out as gay, used some very homophobic lyrics himself.

Tyler was certainly not alone in his hatred of the album *Revival*. The CD was panned and called a failure by many, and yet it went platinum in multiple countries, including the USA. But still, according to *Billboard*, first-week figures for *Revival* were significantly, shockingly lower than that of *The Marshall Mathers LP* 2.

In 2017 at the *BET Hip Hop Awards,* Eminem made an unannounced appearance delivering an aggressive cypher in which he attacked Donald Trump.

When it comes to the "line in the sand," that Eminem

drew, telling Trump fans to forget about him, Marshall has since admitted that if he could do it over again he would "at least reword it" to show more empathy toward *"the people this evil serpent sold the dream to that he's deserted."*

However, while Marshall says he empathizes with fans of Trump, his opinion of Trump himself has not changed. Eminem also expressed some frustration that Trump never responded to *The Storm*. But then the Secret Service turned up to investigate him.

> *"These verses are makin' him a wee bit nervous*
> *And he's too scared to answer me with words*
> *'Cause he knows that he will lyrically get murdered*
> *But I know at least he's heard it*
> *'Cause Agent Orange just sent the Secret Service*
> *To meet in person to see if I really think of*
>   *hurtin' him*
> *Or ask if I'm linked to terrorists*
> *I said, 'Only when it comes to ink and lyricists.'"*

It was not the first time that the Secret Service has investigated Marshall Mathers due to perceived potential "threats" against a president.

In 2003, during George W. Bush's presidency, Eminem released his fourth studio album *Encore*. The smash-hit and fierce diss track *Mosh* on the CD encore encouraged American citizens to go out and vote against President Bush.

But despite the strong wording of *Mosh* in which Eminem declared that "the stars and stripes have been swiped, washed out and wiped and replaced with his own face" it was not *Mosh* that had concerned The Secret Service, but instead a much lesser-known track that only appeared on the deluxe edition of *Encore*, a track called *We As Americans* that featured the line, "*I don't rap for dead presidents/ I'd rather see the president dead.*"

That was apparently enough to trigger a Secret Service first probe into Eminem. But really the line was just a clever play on words about money.

In the end, much like Madonna's declaration, during the Women's March concerning how she had "thought an awful lot about blowing up the Whitehouse," Eminem's words were ultimately not deemed a "credible threat" to the president.

Eminem also admitted in his YouTube interview with Sway Calloway that the Secret Service turned up at his studio again in 2017 to investigate whether Eminem was a threat to a president, this time to President Trump.

But once again, an investigation of a rapper's lyrics proved to be a waste of Secret Service time. The closest line to threatening Trump in his 2017 freestyle *The Storm* was "*Fork and a dagger in this racist 94-year-old grandpa.*" Hardly a "credible threat." Trump is nowhere near 94 years old.

However, the visit certainly did not shut Eminem up, with his stronger denouncement of Trump, coming later on his *Revival* song *"Like Home"* and even on his latest album *Kamikaze*.

In a 2017 concert, Eminem said, *"I don't want to cause any controversy, so I won't say no names. But this mother fucker Donald Trump I can't stand! Before I begin this next song, we would like to request something of you. "When I say Fuck, you say Trump."* He then went on to lead the audience to shout Trump several times."

In a 2017 interview, to publicize *Revival,* Eminem stated: "This is what happens…when I start talking about Trump, I get too flustered in my head. The shit that I wanna say there's too many things that I wanna say at once, so sometimes I start talking, and I'm not able to convey the message, the right way, because I just get flustered and frustrated watching him play to his base that thinks that he cares about them when they're actually the people that he cares about the fucking least.

If you're talking about his core, being a majority white middle class, what I don't understand is, how in the fuck do you feel that you relate to a billionaire, who's never known struggle his entire fucking life.

I will say this though he talks a good one. And if you're in his base, let's say you're going to the rallies, or whatever, you watch him on TV, you hear him talking about this shit. There's part of me that understands ok he's still got them because he's brainwashing them into thinking that something great is going to happen…NOTHING is happening. I'm blessed to have a platform that I can still get attention, as long as I can grab ears that's kind of my intent."

In other interviews such as his *Viper* interview, he has said

"I want our country to be great too, I want it to be the best it can be, but it's not going to be that with him in charge."

Paul Rosenberg (Eminem's long-time manager) has commented, "I saw the results coming in early in the day, and I was hopeful. (But) I (still) thought Trump was gonna win. There was a lot of voter apathy, and it was not good. That made me feel like people weren't gonna turn out enough."

Eminem explained in another 2017 interview, "I called it just from the rallies he was having when he first started running. Because just watching the impact he has, they were fanatics. There is something to be said about the person who really felt like he might do something for them — but he just fucking duped everybody.

I know that Hillary (Clinton) had her flaws, but you know

what? Anything would have been better (than Trump). A fucking turd would have been better as a president. When I (put out *The Storm*), I felt that everybody who was with him at that point. doesn't like my music anyway."

Marshall went on to say, "I get the comparison (between Trump and me) with the non-political-correctness, but other than that, we're polar opposites. He made these people feel like he was really going to do something for them.

It's just so fucking disgusting how divisive his language is, the rhetoric, the Charlottesville shit, just watching it going, 'I can't believe he's saying this.' When he was talking about John McCain, I thought he was done. You're fucking with military veterans; you're talking about a military war hero who was captured and tortured. It just didn't matter. It doesn't matter. And that's some scary shit to me."

In a verse on the *Revival* track, "*Chloraseptic,*" Marshall also talks about his explosive BET Hip-Hop Awards freestyle, *The Storm,* and how it upset some of his fans and made them turn on him. *"Then I took a stand / Went at tan face and practically cut my motherfuckin' fan base in half / And still outsold you."*

During his photoshoot with Rosenberg for Billboard, Eminem spilled more of his thoughts on Trump.

"I know I say a lot of fucked-up shit. But a lot of shit is said in jest, it's tongue-in-cheek, and it has always been that way through my whole career -- saying shit to get a reaction out of people. It's my artistic license to express myself. Last time I checked, Trump isn't an artist and doesn't have an artistic license. I'm not the fuckin' president."

Eminem has complained that Trump has never had the guts to comment on any of his lyrics, but in fact, there was one tweet from Trump on October the 11th 2017.

"I still can't tell if Eminem likes me more or less than his own mother."

Twitter users were quick to pick up on the fact that Trump stole the joke from comedian Anthony Jeselnik who had posted the joke "I still can't tell if Eminem likes Donald Trump more or less than his own mother" only the day before on October 10th.

At 2018 *Coachella*, a number of Trump fans bragged about how they had left the concert early to skip Eminem because he'd "sold out" by not liking the president.

But one need only look back at Eminem's hit 2004 song *Mosh* to see that Eminem has always been a Democrat who wrote equally intense Anti-Bush lyrics.

Having grown up in relative poverty, Eminem has no truck with those that have no sympathy for the poor. In 2017 he reworked a quote from Martin Luther King in his song *Untouchable*

"*Fuck your Republican views. Pull ourselves up by our bootstraps where the fuck are the boots?*"

Eminem was also mocked for his 2017 song *Untouchable,* in which he takes a serious tone discussing police brutality to African Americans.

YouTuber and former rapper Joe Budden, who hosts *The*

Joe Budden Podcast had been slammed by some listeners, for never criticizing Eminem on his show.

The pressure led to Budden calling *Untouchable* the worst song he'd ever heard in his life.

Joe Budden had initially been part of the group *Slaughterhouse,* a hip-hop supergroup consisting of rappers Joe Budden, Joell Ortiz, Kxng Crooked, and Royce da 5'9 and signed to *Interscope.*

Eminem and Paul financially backed the first *Slaughterhouse* album *Welcome to Our House.* But the album was panned by critics.

Shady Records and *Interscope* also spent hundreds of thousands of dollars on a second album *Glass House* that was never released.

Budden claimed the members of Slaughterhouse could never agree on which songs they liked best to put on *Glass House,* and there was much infighting.

Joe Budden, in interviews, asked: "Who got that money?" And implied that Paul Rosenburg and Eminem had taken all the money for the two albums and been unfair to the rap group.

Eminem told Sway, "I hate to say this because I think the guys (in *Slaughterhouse*) are super fucking talented, but the album didn't do much to even recoup the first budget and then we spent hundreds of thousands of dollars on the second album that never came out. What money? What money is he talking about? I don't know if I made a dime off Slaughterhouse, and I don't care. It actually hurt my feelings a lot… (that such a talented group's album didn't sell.)"

Budden has a reported net worth of six million, so he's not doing too badly.

Joe also said on his podcast that he wasn't interested in money for *Slaughterhouse* and that he just wanted respect and was doing it for the love of hip-hop. Unlike the other members of the group, whom he claimed were doing it for money and fame. Yet ironically, Joe Budden appears to be the only member of Slaughterhouse complaining about how little the first album made.

Budden also claimed that he has been a better rapper than Eminem for the entire decade between 2008-2018 because he writes about "concepts." While Eminem (in his opinion) just has clever rhymes and isn't writing about issues.

However, the irony is that when Eminem did write on a serious topic, Budden attacked Marshall's right to even speak police brutality.

Budden also criticized Eminem for expressing his political views through the cover of *Revival* with the facepalm behind the flag. And he attacked a whole album he hadn't even heard based on the album cover, one song, and the tracklist names.

Joe complained on his podcast that he suffered dealing with complicated workplace politics after signing to *Interscope*.

Budden said that within *Slaughterhouse,* there was infighting over who got to do verses in which songs and that Interscope often cut his own verse to make songs shorter. "Somebody's verse had to go. Imagine that competition in the studio racing to the booth. It's nasty, it's nasty, it's nasty, it's nasty. I don't want no part of it."

Joe expressed a lot of bitterness regarding the cut verses on songs he claimed he had the original concept for.

Apparently, producers cut more of Budden's verses than those of any other member of Slaughterhouse.

Budden said, "you know what Joe's gonna do every-time you try and contaminate his idea? Exit! Exit stage left." This explains why *Glass House* was never released.

In a live stream, Kxng Crooked blamed the Slaughterhouse break-up on Joe Budden's lack of communication and poor decision making.

When asked why he thought it was *his* verses that were cut from *Slaughterhouse* CDs by *Interscope*, Budden has no answer saying that he "can't speak for people."

However, both Eminem and Joe Budden have admitted in interviews that the two of them have never been close. This could leave one to wonder, did Paul and others at Interscope, choose to cut Budden's verses because Budden didn't have as tight a friendship as the other artists of *Slaughterhouse* with Eminem? Or because Budden just wasn't as popular with producers down at *Interscope*?

Asked by Sway, if the Slaughterhouse album *Glass House* would ever be released, Eminem is tactful.

"I can't answer to that. But I just want to say that apart from the Joe shit, I think Slaughterhouse is one of the greatest groups ever formed.... I wish their first album had connected to more people than it did....to this day me and Paul are like "what the fuck happened?"

Of Eminem's political song *Untouchable*- a song written to draw attention to police brutality, Joe Budden said "Trash! This is one of the worst songs I have ever heard. You will not use the plight of black people ... *Interscope* or whoever the fuck is behind that.... to sell a fucking record, and widen your fucking profit margin!"

This statement makes a lot of assumptions. The first obviously false assumption is that *Interscope* is controlling Eminem and telling him what to write about. This seems an absurd idea considering Eminem's level of celebrity, financial success, and power in 2017 at the time the song *Untouchable* was released. As Eminem said in his 2018 song *Fall*

> *All I know is I wrote every single word of*
> *Everything I ever murdered*
> *Time to separate the sheep from goats (yeah)*
> *And I got no faith in your writers, I don't believe in ghosts*

Eminem has always written his own lyrics and come up with his own concepts.

The second assumption that Eminem doesn't have the right to express his opinion about an issue that affects dozens upon dozens of his friends is also a strange and questionable one.

The third demonstrably false assumption Joe Budden makes in his statement is that the song *Untouchable* was just written to "sell a fucking record, and widen a fucking profit margin." The reason that this appears to be false is that *Untouchable* was not one of the main songs used to promote the album the big songs with music videos were *Walk on Water*, *River*, and *Framed*.

Admittedly *Untouchable* was released early without a video as a promotional single, but still, the assumption that Eminem would write about a serious subject, purely "to increase his profit margin," seems rather unfair.

According to Joe Budden, Eminem apparently isn't allowed to care about an issue because he's had many close friends who've been harassed? He can't try to promote awareness of a societal problem that bothers him because of the color of his skin?

Eminem hit back at Budden in his *Sway* interview saying: "When I'm out here flying around to different places, and doing interviews and trying to use my platform to pump up *Slaughterhouse*, and you're using your platform to fucking trash me, and I'm one of the things, that keeps this ship moving....you don't owe me nothing, but I've never got on a fucking interview and been like "Joe Budden's shit is fucking trash". That last album he put out is fucking trash! So that's kind of the attitude I took to this whole album *Kamikaze* is like, "alright, what if I give my opinion about them?"

Joe Budden accused *Interscope* of encouraging Eminem to use race as a hot button political issue just to increase profit margins. But according to *HotNewHipHop,* Paul Rosenberg accused Joe Budden of using both himself (Rosenberg) and Eminem "just to get a little pop for your podcast," implying that Joe Budden was using Eminem and Paul to "increase his fucking profit margins."

Paul hit back at Budden even harder on *Ebro in the Morning,* saying: "You're finished, just like your career, one hot song fifteen years ago."

Rosenberg appears to be referencing Budden's popular song *Pump It Up.*

Joe Budden has, however, defended another one of Eminem's political tracts, *The Storm* admitting, "I...think that we need that sentiment from white people, and I appreciate that."

Hilariously on his podcast, Budden attempted to walk back some of his criticisms of Eminem by saying he has loved Eminem ever since he heard him say, "Hey kids do you like eyelids?" Something Eminem never said!

The line is actually

Hi, kids, do you like violence? (Yeah, yeah, yeah)
Wanna see me stick nine-inch nails through each one
  of my eyelids?

Somehow Joe Budden managed to misquote Eminem's very first breakout hit *My Name Is* in a room full of hip-hop fans gathered for his podcast. Only one of them muttered a correction of the line under his breath.

To be fair however, when it comes to his criticisms of the song *Untouchable*, it seems Budden may have been most angry about the fact that the beat and hook for the song sounded so terrible, and that he thought *Interscope* may have been encouraging Eminem to release a poorly done song on a political hot button in order to gain attention for the album.

When Budden said "disgraceful," he may have simply meant the music more than anything else.

Budden has also said that he thinks Eminem is one of the most color blind (in terms of race) white men he's ever known.

EVEN IN HIS EARLY DAYS, Eminem was controversial in politics.

In 1999 while Bill Clinton was still in office, Eminem released the song *Role Model* with the lyrics.

> *(Oh no) So if I said I never did drugs*
> *That would mean I lie and get fucked more than the*
> *President does*
> *Hilary Clinton tried to slap me and call me a pervert*
> *I ripped her fuckin' tonsils out and fed her sherbet*

In the year 2000, Eminem continued to make fun of the President for the Lewinsky scandal and pointed out the hypocrisy of the constant requests from the FCC to tone down his lyrics, considering what everyone knew about the president.

I'm sorry, there must be a mix-up
You want me to fix up lyrics
While our President gets his dick sucked?

He even made fun of Bill Clinton again many years after his presidency with the line in 2013's *Rap God*.

My pen'll go off when I half-cock it
Got a fat knot from that rap profit
Made a livin' and a killin' off it
Ever since Bill Clinton was still in office
With Monica Lewinsky feelin' on his nutsack
I'm an MC still as honest.

But making fun of Democrats sex scandals was nothing compared to his troubles with the Republican Party.

In 2001 Eminem was the subject of a congressional hearing although he was not present. Republicans pushed for the record industry to expand its warning labels for parents because of Eminem's lyrics. In particular, the song *Kill You* in which he jokes about raping his own mother.

Addressing Mathers' lyrics and music, Lynn Cheney the vice-second Lady of the United States from 2001 to 2009, said, "Eminem is not the first rapper to revel in violent misogyny, but he has taken hatred of women and depictions of degrading and violating them" to new levels.

In a way, Eminem hits back at such accusations in the song itself rapping

You're goddamn right, bitch, and now it's too late
I'm triple platinum and tragedies happened in two
    states
I invented violence, you vile venomous volatile bitches

Vain Vicodin, vrin!
Texas Chainsaw left his brains all
Danglin' from his neck while his head barely hangs on
Blood, guts, guns, cuts
Knives, lives, wives, nuns, sluts

Here in the song *Kill You* itself, Eminem points out how violent movies can be (*Texas Chainsaw*), and yet no one is picketing outside the cinema showing horror movies the same way they were protesting his music. Eminem frequently writes horror-core hip hop songs, the musical equivalent of a horror novel or film.

He underlines this in another song.

And last week I seen this Schwarzenegger movie
Where he's shootin' all sorts of these motherfuckers
    with an Uzi
I see these three little kids up in the front row
Screaming "Go!" with their 17-year-old uncle
I'm like, guidance?!
Ain't they got the same moms and dads
Who got mad when I asked if they liked violence?

More recently some conservative bloggers freaked out over Eminem's video and song that mentioned putting Ivanka Trump in the trunk of his car, calling the song a threat, seemingly unaware what a frequent theme this kind of thing has been on Eminem's albums, or that Eminem is known as a "horrorcore" rapper.

In 2018 *BuzzFeed News* filed a *Freedom of Information Act* request with the Secret Service to find out if agents really were sent to speak with Eminem regarding the lyrics from *Framed*.

BuzzFeed uncovered that Marshall had indeed had a third visit from the Secret Service.

The official documents revealed that an employee from the tabloid website TMZ, had emailed The Secret Service, saying: "I want to know if your agency is investigating Eminem for his threatening lyrics about First Daughter Ivanka Trump?" The documents do not reveal the agency received correspondence from any other individual regarding the song.

The documents also noted, "This is not the first time MATHERS made threatening comments towards POTUS and his family. In June 2017, MATHERS freestyled comments that were threatening in nature towards POTUS."

The documents obtained from The Secret Service also show the agency's Protective Intelligence and Assessment Division conducted a background check on Eminem and started to arrange an interview with the rapper through his attorneys.

At the interview with Eminem and his lawyers, Marshall was questioned a second time concerning his *BET* freestyle rap; next, he was questioned about the lyrics regarding Ivanka in *Framed*.

Marshall was also questioned about the Trump related lyrics in the song *Like Home*.

At one point in the interview, documents show that Marshall started to rap out loud.

Possibly he did this to show the sonically appealing quality of the lyrics since it can be assumed, they were being read out to him in a monotone, making them sound more threatening than the reality of the track's entertainment value.

The agents then questioned Eminem about "fan mail that may include threats or unusual interest items due to his songs."

A good portion of the document was redacted. So not everything that went on in the interview is known.

The interview was discussed two days later at a Secret Service meeting, and once again, it was determined that a case against Marshall would not be "NON-REFERRED" to a federal prosecutor.

We can assume Eminem and his attorneys know how to handle these meetings effectively, and they clearly convinced The Secret Service that Marshall was not a threat to either Ivanka or her father.

The theme of a dead woman in the trunk of Eminem's car began with the song *97 Bonnie and Clyde* on the *Slim Shady LP*, in which he takes his toddler daughter to the beach, with the body of his wife (her mother) in the trunk of his car. A chilling song that plays with dichotomy of a man being filled with rage and murderous feelings against his wife for cheating on him while being filled with love for the child they had together.

> *C'mon hai-hai, we goin' to the beach*
> *Grab a couple of toys and let da-da strap you in the car seat*
> *Oh, where's mama? she's takin a little nap in the trunk*
> *Oh, that smell (whew!) da-da musta runned over a skunk*
> *Now I know what you're thinkin', it's kind of late to go swimmin'*
> *But you know your mama, she's one of those type of women*
> *That do crazy things, and if she don't get her way, she'll throw a fit*
> *Don't play with da-da's toy knife, honey, let go of it (no!)*

The female body in the trunk of his car is then repeated in the even more famous song, *Stan,* where Eminem's stalker Stan copies the *'97 Bonnie and Clyde* song, by putting his own pregnant girlfriend in the trunk of his car before driving it off a bridge.

Eminem then went hardcore on this idea with his 2009 almost pure horrorcore serial killer themed album *Relapse,* where he joked about killing numerous female celebrities, including Lindsay Lohan and Britney Spears. So, this was really not a threat against Ivanka Trump to anyone familiar with his work.

Eminem commented in an interview, *"People don't understand that it's not really about them. I've never met these people personally it's more just like pulling names out of a hat, and if your name rhymes with something good...."*

The broadcaster responded *"But you can see how if you mention Sarah Palin people are going to think 'Oh he wants to make a statement about Sarah Palin.'"*

Eminem responded with lustful energy *"Well, I do. I want to nail her."*

The only time Eminem mentioned Sarah Palin in a song was the following in his 2009 song *We Made You.*

Well, I can be as gentle and as smooth as a gentleman
Give me my Ventolin inhaler and two Xenadrine
And I'll invite Sarah Palin out to dinner, then
Nail her, baby, say hello to my little friend!

Purely all about the rhyme.

In 2017 Sarah Palin chose to comment on Eminem's song the *River* tweeting "Eminem's New Song Does Something Liberals Won't Like: Apologizes to an Aborted Baby! "

Palin then linked to an article with the same title and

saying, "love it!" Leading to derision on her twitter thread from Eminem fans.

Eminem associate Denaun M. Porter, better known by his stage name Mr. Porter, clarified for fans, that there was no baby, and that Eminem only made up a story, about having a fling, and accidentally getting a woman pregnant.

Another thing many people missed about the song is that River is a retelling of Bruce Springsteen's song *The River*.

The River is a song of sadness concerning a marriage that only happened because of a baby. Eminem writes a different *River* song about the baby being aborted instead of the shotgun wedding of Springsteen's song.

Eminem's song *River* is merely a story about regret over a short-lived fling and an abortion and very unlikely to be a pro-life advert from Eminem.

But Eminem is a talented marketer, and he probably wanted people to be confused to generate buzz.

Marshall and actress Sarati, who starred in the *River* video, even deliberately went into a hotel together to get caught by Paparazzi in an attempt to go viral, leading to much speculation concerning whom the new woman was in Eminem's life. (In fact, they were never dating.)

Another interesting point concerning Eminem and politics is that his mother, Debbie Mathers, holds directly opposing political views in terms of Trump.

In fact, Debbie Mathers is a big Trump fan with a secret twitter account that the author of this book discovered and will tell you more about in the coming chapters.

CHAPTER THREE

A lot of people ask me, am I afraid of death?
Hell yeah, I'm afraid of death
I don't want to die yet

Nine Times Eminem Nearly Died
(*Keep winking, and blowin' kisses 'cause you're flirting with death.*)

MOST PEOPLE WHO KNOW ABOUT EMINEM KNOW THAT HIS early life was hard. But they may not know that his life has been in danger many times, including after his fame.

1) In 1982 Marshall was nearly beaten to death by a "fat kid named DeAngelo Bailey" in elementary school who gave him a cerebral hemorrhage that doctors initially believed he would not recover from. Doctors even told Debbie that Marshall would need to be institutionalized.

"Way before my baby daughter Hailie.

*I was harassed daily
by this fat kid named DeAngelo Bailey,
an eighth-grader who acted obnoxious
'cause his father boxes."*

Eminem told *Rolling Stone*, "I was in fourth grade, and he was in sixth. Everything in the song is true: One day he came in the bathroom, I was pissing, and he beat the shit out of me. Pissed all over myself. But that's not how I got really fucked up. During recess one winter D'Angelo Bailey — no one called him D'Angelo — came running from across the yard and hit me so hard into this snowbank that I blacked out."

Marshall was sent home. He was taken to the hospital because his ear was bleeding. "He had a cerebral hemorrhage and was in and out of consciousness for five days," Debbie Mathers explains in her book. "The doctors had given up on him, but I wouldn't give up on my son." One doctor told Debbie Marshall would never get better and that she would need to institutionalize him.

But after five days, Eminem woke up from his coma and said: "I can spell elephant."

In 2001, DeAngelo Baily was interviewed about the subject by *Rolling Stone* and ruined his own chances in his later court case by admitting to the bullying and assaults, "There was a bunch of us that used to mess with him. You know, bully-type things. We was (sic) having fun. Sometimes he'd fight back — depended on what mood he'd be in. We flipped him right on his head at recess. When we didn't see him moving, we took off running. We lied and said he slipped on the ice."

"He was small, plus he had a big mouth," recalled Bailey, a laborer with four children. He told *Salon* Magazine that he has signed autographs for teeny-bopper fans and that he had to disconnect his phone.

Bailey lost the court battle, where he tried to sue Eminem for mentioning him in the song. Today Bailey brags about his bullying even further, quoting the line *"who acted obnoxious, cause his father boxes."* Now I Box like my father," on his Twitter profile. There are also several fake D'Angelo Bailey's on twitter.

Whereas previously Bailey tried a rapping career, the bully has now decided to follow in his father's footsteps as a boxer.

Macomb County Circuit Judge Deborah Servitto, who was the judge in the D'Angelo Bailey versus Eminem case, regular opinion, wrote a rap verse explaining her ruling (in addition to a regular opinion.)

"Bailey thinks he's entitled to some monetary gain/ Because Eminem used his name in vain," she wrote. *"The lyrics are stories no one would take as fact/ They're an exaggeration of a childish act/ It is, therefore, this court's ultimate position/ That Eminem is entitled to summary disposition."*

This meant the court agreed with Eminem's lawyers that Bailey had no case because there were no facts at issue. Only obvious fiction.

Bailey also bragged to reporters that he must have really messed Eminem up and got in Marshall's head for him to write that line, harming his case and making Bailey look even more obnoxious.

2) Child abuse claims the lives of three children daily in the United States; however, one form of child abuse frequently goes undiagnosed, and that is Munchausen Syndrome by Proxy. A condition Eminem fans may recall Marshall mentioning in the song *Cleaning Out My Closet*.

MSBP is a hidden and deceitful abuse whereby a caretaker fabricates information to make a dependent person appear mentally or physically ill, in order to gain attention. Munchausen by Proxy Syndrome is a deadly disorder. Many of the victims of this condition become disabled or die though the statistics on exactly how many are hard to come by.

Eminem's mother allegedly had Munchausen's Syndrome by Proxy. She admits in her own book that she was diagnosed with the syndrome. However, she emphatically denies she had the condition and claims she was framed by Nathan's school.

Debbie Mathers asserts that the symptoms of abuse that social workers uncovered were not caused by herself but were actually caused by school bullies.

According to Debbie Nathan's school took revenge on her because she had reported them to child protective services for allowing Nathan to be beaten up in their care. She also claims they framed her because she had threatened to sue them for Nathan's injuries.

Eminem's little half-brother Nathan was removed from her care by the state of Michigan for this reason allegedly and put into foster care where he remained for one year.

The song *My Mom* is clearly an exaggeration, similar to the D'Angelo Bailey related song *Brain Damage*.

However, Eminem dos appear to be serious in his claim that Debbie would sometimes give her boys Valium in an attempt to sedate them, and make them more manageable.

The reason one can speculate that he is not joking regarding this claim is that he mentions it in at least three different songs, including two serious songs, and not just in the exaggerated horrorcore song *My Mom*.

Quotes in his songs relating to the Munchausen's Syndrome by Proxy include

*Now I would never diss my own momma just to get
   recognition
Take a second to listen for who you think this record is
   dissing
But put yourself in my position, just try to envision
Witnessing your momma popping prescription pills in
   the kitchen
Bitching that someone's always going through her
   purse and shit's missing
Going through public housing systems, victim of
   Munchhausen's Syndrome
My whole life, I was made to believe I was sick when I
   wasn't.*

From *Cleaning Out My Closet*

The song *My Mom* clearly has a lot of crazy exaggerations and hyperbole. But amongst the embellishments are what seem like some serious lines

*"Here, want a snack? You hungry, you fuckin' brat?
Look at that, it's a Xanax, take it and take a nap,
   eat it."
But I don't need it "Well fuck it then, break it up
Take a little piece and beat it before you wake
   Nathan up."*

Later in the same song, he says

*"So, every day I'd have at least three stomachaches
Now tell me what kind of mother would want to
   see her
Son grow up to be an under-a-fuckin'-chiever?"*

And the lines

> *"Mrs. Mathers, your son has been huffing ether*
> *Either that or the motherfucker's been puffin' reefer"*
> *But all this huffin' and puffin' wasn't what it was either*
> *It was neither, I was buzzing, but it wasn't what she thought*

These lines seem to indicate that while Marshall may be joking about Valium being in literally everything he ate and drank as a kid, but that his mother may have tried to sedate her active little boys with her medication.

What really caps this off is lines in what the media liked to call Eminem's "apology to his mother" 2014's song *Headlights*. Eminem does not back down concerning these accusations in this peace-making song that Nathan asked him to write for their mom.

But I'm sorry mama for 'Cleaning Out My Closet,' at the time I was angry

> *Rightfully maybe so, never meant that far to take it though, 'cause*
> *Now I know it's not your fault, and I'm not making jokes*
> *That song I no longer play at shows and I cringe every time it's on the radio*
> *And I think of Nathan being placed in a home*
> *And all the medicine you fed us*
> *And how I just wanted you to taste your own, but*
> *Now the medications takin' over and your mental states deteriorating slow*
> *And I'm way too old to cry, that shit's painful though*

But ma, I forgive you, so does Nathan yo
All you did, all you said, you did your best to raise
   us both
Foster care that cross you bare, few may be as heavy
   as yours
But I love you Debbie Mathers

"The medicine they were fed us" means the prescription pills, as mentioned in the song *My Mom*.

The song *My Mom* is very much like the song *Brain Damage,* which was about the severe beating Marshall received from DeAngelo Bailey at the age of nine. In both songs, Eminem greatly exaggerates something dire in his life for comic effect and adds surreal elements.

Valium was in everything, food that I ate
The water that I drank, fucking peas on my plate
She sprinkled just enough of it to season my steak

Debbie denies any of this is true. While Debbie does admit to being given the diagnosis of Munchausen Syndrome by proxy in her autobiographical book *My Son Marshall, My Son Eminem,* she denies the diagnosis was accurate.

In her book, Debbie also admits being charged with abuse and neglect of Eminem's half-brother Nathan. She explains in her book that she was charged in a court of law, but claims she was innocent, set up by the school who were allowing Nathan to be beaten by bullies just as Marshall was years before him.

Debbie took a plea bargain on abuse and neglect of Nathan; she claims Nathan begged her to so.

Debbie also claims that she was the one who called child protective services to complain that Nathan's teachers were allowing bullies to beat him and staff to harm him. She says the school turned this around on her in vengeance.

The school alleged that Debbie had taken Nathan to ten or more doctors. But Debbie claims she proved that the school was mistaken and that her regular family doctor backed her up in court.

A social worker told doctors that Debbie "exhibited a very suspicious and almost paranoid personality."

School officials at Nathan's school also alleged that Debbie accused neighbors of beating Nathan, blowing up her mailbox, and killing her dog in a satanic ritual. They added that she told them video cameras were monitoring her from trees outside her house and that enemies had sent her a tarantula in the mail.

It seems Debbie may possibly have had some drug-induced psychosis.

Don DeMarc, who dated Debbie in the last 70s and early 80s, also told Salon that Mathers-Briggs endured nagging pain, stemming from being hit by a car with a drunken driver. (Something Debbie also claims in her book.) DeMarc went on to say, "She complained of headaches, backaches, and toothaches," he says. "She always seems to be in pain. She's always looking for pain pills."

Marshall's former co-workers at *Gilbert's Lodge* remember her calling him constantly at the restaurant, demanding to speak to her son, even during peak times when he couldn't come to the phone.

St. Clair Shores police have also said that she often summoned them with unfounded complaints concerning the neighbors.

Debbie was able to successfully sue Nathan's father, Fred, for child support. Fred Samra Jr., later told *Salon* Magazine: "Debbie is lying about not doing drugs and stuff. I won't say any more." Of Eminem, he said, "You would not believe the shit he has been through."

3) Shortly after the trial against Debbie in 1996, Eminem was fired from his job as a short-order cook at the restaurant *Gilbert's Lodge*.

His album *Infinite* that he'd put so much time and effort and money into the same year was a flop. These events led to a suicide attempt.

The album sold a little under five hundred copies after pressing up 1000. One song from the album was played on local radio, but he was mocked by the disc jockeys for his white skin. Marshall was also compared to Vanilla Ice, which he found horrifying. Other critics claimed he sounded too much like New York rappers AZ and Nas.

As Eminem has explained in interviews, no one wanted to be compared to anyone else in rap during that period. Even though he loved AZ and Nas, he hated being criticized for sounding too similar to them. (Marshall discusses how that seems to have changed in the Sway interview and how the change influenced his lyrics on *Kamikaze*.)

Infinite was also mocked on the radio for being too pleasant and upbeat. The only song from the album that got airplay was a love song he'd written for Kim entitled *Searchin*. The difference between the loving lyrics to this song about Kim, compared to other songs about Kim, such as *97 Bonnie and Clyde*, *Kim,* and *Puke,* is shocking.

> *The way your lips sparkle and glare in the sun,*
> *You got your hair in a bun, no matter what you're wearing you stun,*
> *Cause you're comparing to none, I wanna share in the fun,*

I feel a passionate lust when I'm imagining just us
*   alone at last with a touch,*
I see you grasping to trust, but my intentions are
*   good,*
The seed is passing in dust,
I'm not asking to rush and answer immediately,
I just wanna be there for you and you to be there
*   for me,*
If you agree to repeat after me, I Love You (I love you
*   baby)*
Cause I need you to see.
How much I'm eager to be,
Your man legally wed,
Your love's keeping me fed,

The sweetness was mocked. The radio hosts also laughed at Eminem for thanking his wife and mother for their support.

Searchin was the last true love song Eminem would ever write though he has since written multiple dark and cynical parodies of love songs. Songs that tongue-in-cheek glorify domestic violence.

By October 1996, Marshall had broken up with Kim once again and was living with some friends in an apartment. When another friend offered them cheaper rent but lied, and pocketed all their cash, they were thrown out, locked out, and all their stuff was thrown on the lawn, Eminem was homeless and went to a homeless shelter where he penned the songs *If I had* and *Rock Bottom*.

Fat Joe, the founder of hip-hop record label *Terror Squad* recently recalled the desperate Marshall of this era in an interview with WEDR 99.1 FM.

"Eminem gave me his demo like… six different times. And everywhere I went there was this little white boy, and he kept giving me his demo. He was like 'yo listen to my music, I am telling you, I am nice, I'm nice, I'm nice.' And I never really...I didn't do it. I didn't listen."

Just before Christmas, Eminem was rehired at *Gilbert's Lodge*. He intended to do extra shifts over the holiday to buy Hailie her birthday and Christmas presents. (As is often the case with work of a short-order cook being hired, fired and rehired was a problem with the job.)

Five days before Christmas, a new chef fired him yet again. He told Marshall he was firing him because he hadn't worn his chef shirt one day. Eminem had been working there for most of three years, and that's what he was fired for, five days before Christmas. Eminem told *NME* magazine that he'd had forty-five dollars left.

But Kim had a new job, and she had money. Kim had told everyone the new job was as a receptionist at a health spa, but Debbie Mathers claims she visited the "health spa" once and that it was really a strip club with lap dances.

Regardless one way or another Kim was able to buy Hailie Christmas presents. Eminem mentions this in his popular song, *Mockingbird*.

> *It's funny*
> *I remember back one year when daddy had no money*
> *Mommy wrapped the Christmas presents up*
> *And stuck 'em under the tree and said some of 'em were from me*
> *Cause daddy couldn't buy 'em*
> *I'll never forget that Christmas I sat up the whole night crying*
> *Cause daddy felt like a bum*

Through it, all though, Eminem had had hope for a bright

future. A man that he knew for a fact worked at a major label had promised him a deal after hearing *Infinite*.

Then on Christmas Eve, a friend told Marshall that the man who'd promised him a deal was, in reality, a fraud. The man was a braggart who only worked in the label's mailroom. Marshall was crushed. That night he recorded the song *Rock Bottom*.

> *That's rock bottom, when this life makes you mad enough to kill*
> *That's rock bottom, when you want somethin' bad enough to steal*
> *That's rock bottom, when you feel like you've had it up to here*
> *'Cause you mad enough to scream, but you sad enough to tear.*

During a break in taping the song, Marshall decided to kill himself.

He told *Music365* magazine that that Christmas Eve, he felt sure he wasn't going to get a deal no matter what.

Marshall took 20 Tylenol 3 in the course of 2 hours. And an hour later threw them all up.

4) Eminem's life was also often at risk wandering around his own dangerous neighborhood. One day he was shot at while walking home from Kim's house and narrowly missed being hit.

The 'hoods he lived in as a teen were always rough, and Marshall frequently got jumped and beaten for being skinny and white. But that day walking home from visiting his girlfriend, he was actually shot at and managed to duck the bullets and survive.

5) According to Eminem's former bodyguard, Byron

Williams- Suge Knight, the founder and CEO of rap label *Death Row Records*, the biggest hip-hop record label of the 1990s allegedly tried to have Eminem killed on two separate occasions.

Suge was furious that Dr. Dre had left *Death Row Records* to form his own company rival label Aftermath Entertainment. And was even more furious that Dre's label was having such phenomenal success with Eminem.

Suge was a convicted felon and member of the Bloods gang and security guard Big Naz claimed that gang members from The Bloods gang from Compton threatened to assassinate Eminem at *The Source Hip Hop Awards* saying that Surge from *Death Row* sent them.

6) The second time that it happened, Eminem went to perform in Honolulu, and again, Big Naz said everyone went into lockdown with twenty Honolulu police officers protecting all the crew on the show because death threats had been made against Eminem by people claiming to have been sent by Surge and the ironically named Death Row.

7) Eminem allegedly pulled a gun on his former bodyguard, a furious Byron Williams who (unbeknownst to Marshall) already had his hand on a pistol in his pocket.) Williams was beside himself with rage because Eminem's manager Paul Rosenburg had allegedly reversed a promised Christmas bonus, out of spite after Williams told Marshall, Rosenburg was stealing from both himself (Williams) and from Marshall. The incident might have ended tragically.

8) *Murder Inc Records* founded by Irv and Chris Gotti allegedly planned violence against Eminem and 50 cent. Federal prosecutors recently accused Irving "Gotti" Lorenzo of receiving "street protection" from Kenneth "Supreme" McGriff in exchange for laundering money into *Murder Inc*.

In the year 2000, 50 cent (real name Curtis Jackson) was

shot nine times outside his grandmother's home. Jackson was shot in the hand, arm, hip, both legs, chest, and left cheek. A fragment of a bullet remains lodged to the inside of his mouth, causing a slight slur.

It is alleged that 50 Cent's unreleased track, Ghetto Qu'ran, was the reason for his attempted murder.

The song, which leaked in early 2000, revolves around lyrics about drug dealers from the 1980s in Jackson's home town of South Jamaica, Queens – specifically, he mentioned Kenneth McGriff.

McGriff was a notorious convicted drug trafficker. According to *Billboard*, federal investigators have alleged McGriff organized the shooting fearing 50 cent's song revealed too much about his criminal activity.

After signing 50 cent Eminem became aware that his own life might be at risk from the association. This was one of the reasons he wrote the song *Like Toy Soldiers*

> *But I'm so busy bein' pissed off, I don't stop to think*
> *That we just inherited 50's beef with Murder Inc.*
> *And he's inherited mine, which is fine, ain't like either*
>   *of us*
> *Mind*

Later in the song saying:

> *But I ain't tryna have none of my people hurt or*
>   *murdered*
> *It ain't worth it,*
> *I can't think of a perfecter way to word it*

Like Toy Soldiers was an attempt by Eminem permanently walk away from some of these potentially life-threatening beefs he'd become involved in and raise awareness of how dangerous rap beefs could become.

9) Eminem ended up in the hospital from his drug overdose between *Encore* and *Relapse*. Marshall has written about this near-death experience in a number of his songs, including *Déjà Vu* on *Relapse*. He also goes into great depth on the songs *Castle* and *Arose* from his 2017 album *Revival*.

Eminem started taking drugs seriously in 2001. As the pressures of fame grew and his relationship with Kim went on a roller coaster of love and hate, Marshall slipped further into alcoholism, addiction to sleeping pills, and prescription painkillers.

In December 2007, he finally overdosed and nearly died.

Eminem began taking drugs on tour in 2001. But after his second divorce from Kim and the death of his best friend Proof in 2006, he started taking pretty much any drug that anyone would give him.

And many people were eager to give him drugs. He had many hangers-on willing to provide him with pills for free. Uppers to help him work, downers so he could go to sleep. He talks about those days jokingly on the song *Hello* on *Relapse*

> *My equilibrium's off must be the lithium*
> *I don't need to buy any drugs, man, people give*
>   *me 'em*
> *It just becomes every day, extra-curriculum*
> *No reason, in particular, it was strictly fun*
> *A fifth of rum and two bottles of 151*
> *Fifty-one people asleep in my damn living room.*

Marshall also told *Vibe* magazine that "doctors to the rich" got such a kick of showing off to people that they knew

Eminem, that they ring his house at random and offer him whatever prescription he might want. Marshall could hear that these doctors were showing off to people in the background that they could phone Eminem.

On *60 minutes,* Eminem explained that he hadn't known or cared what the blue pills even were. Someone gave them to him, and they turned out to be methadone. The last thing he remembered was saying goodnight to his three daughters. He was found collapsed in the bathroom. Alaina was 14. Hailie was 12 years old at the time, and little Whitney was only five.

The year before Eminem's near-death experience, DeShaun Dupree Holton, known professionally as Proof, was shot three times and killed by Mario Etheridge.

The shooting occurred during a dispute over a drunken game of billiards. Etheridge managed to convince authorities that it was self-defense and that Proof had shot another man first.

All who knew Proof doubt the veracity of this. Unfortunately, Proof did have a blood alcohol content that was 0.32, four times the legal DUI limit at the time both shootings occurred. Proof's close friend Reginald "Mudd" Moore, who was with him at the nightclub that night alledged to XXL magazine that he'd seen Etheridge kill both his cousin and Proof, but the authorities did not charge him with murder.

Marshall first met Proof at age sixteen years old. DeShaun was a year younger. Eminem details the first meeting on the song *Yellow Brick Road* on his 2004 album *Encore.*

That's about the time I first met Proof when poof he'd carry on the set
Set eyes born in and out some flyers, he was doin' some talent shows

> *At Centerline, I had told him to stop by and check this*
> * out sometime*
> *He looked at me like I'm out my mind shook his head*
> * like white boys don't know how to rhyme*
> *I spit out a line and rhymed birthday with first place*
> *And we both had the same rhymes that sound alike*
> *We was on the same shit that Big Daddy Kane shit*
> * with compound syllables sound combined*
> *From that day we was down to ride somehow, we*
> * knew we'd meet again somewhere down the line*

DeShaun then really warmed his heart for life when one day the fifteen-year-old threw a pair of white Nikes at Marshall.

Eminem asked what they were for, and DeShaun said: "Cause I'm tired of you wearing them dirty ass shoes." The younger boy had bought Marshall brand new shoes, his favorite brand, out of his own part-time job money.

Marshall's second divorce to Kim was finalized on April 5th, 2006 just days before his best friend Proof's death on April 11th, 2006 the double whammy must have been one hell of a blow to the already prescription drug-addicted Marshall.

Regarding Proof's death, it appears Kim really did not understand what Marshall was going through at the time at all.

In interviews with local radio in 2006 and 2007, Kim infuriated Eminem by telling them that he was having problems with prescription drugs still. And that it had been part of the reason their second marriage only lasted a few months. She also claimed she had been hoping to go to counseling but instead had divorce papers served to her at the door.

In 2005, *Kim told Mojo in the Morning*, "He's having

problems with, you know, his problem that he had. I was hoping we could get counseling and work it out, you know? I hope in his best interest that he does return to rehab."

Eminem's publicist fired off a response from Eminem "Her allegations regarding my status post-rehab are both untrue and unfortunate." Marshall has since admitted that this was a lie and that he failed at rehab many times.

In another *Mojo in the Morning* interview, Kim told how the Eminem of that time was behaving in a very strange manner. Asked what Hailie would have to say about how Eminem was acting, she said, "Weird. She'd say he's acting weird. That's what the kids ask me every single day 'why is dad acting so weird?'"

Kim claimed that in 2006 (actually in the months after Proof died) that when she brought Hailie around for court designated visits that the back door would be unlocked, they'd come in and Eminem would be asleep in his bedroom.

Eminem seems to confirm this himself, singing disparagingly about his 2006 behavior on his 2009 album *Relapse* in his song *Déjà vu*

> *And you'd think that with all I have at stake*
> *Look at my daughter's face*
> *"Mommy, something is wrong with dad I think*
> *He's acting weird again, he's really beginning to scare me*
> *Won't shave his beard again and he pretends he doesn't hear me*
> *And all he does is eat Doritos and Cheetos*
> *And he just fell asleep in his car eating 3 Musketeers in the rear seat."*

Kim said she'd end up staying in his house with Hailie

and Alaina during the court-ordered visit, while Eminem was asleep passed out on prescription drugs, and that she could not wake him for some of their visits. This was Eminem at one of his lowest points.

And after his "rock bottom," in December 2007, where he nearly died, he began the long road to recovery and sobriety that has lasted twelve years.

The 2006 behavior was devasting to his family, though.

In this interview, Kim expressed confusion regarding the video for the December 2006 hit *When I'm Gone* because of the lines (and accompanied video hugging)

Alarm clock's ringing, there's birds singin'
It's spring and Hailie's outside swingin'
I walk right up to Kim and kiss her tell her I miss her
Hailie just smiles and winks at her little sister

The videos for *When I'm Gone* and *Mockingbird* were confusing to fans who previously knew Kim from songs like *97 Bonnie and Clyde* and the even more violent song *Kim*.

There is so much love shown to Kim in these two songs. On the radio, she said, "And his little video *When I'm Gone* nothing like that is going on!"

What Kim seemed to fail to understand was how long the process between writing a song and a music video took. Clearly, the song and the concept for the video were written at the time Kim and Marshall had rekindled their romance and were planning their second marriage. *Mockingbird* was also originally written at that time. By the time the videos for these songs came out, the romantic reunion was well over.

Kim explained that she Hailie and Whitney were going to be in the original video for *When I'm Gone,* but Kim had found a bunch of loose pills in the bedroom that the children might have stumbled on.

Kim was concerned about the number of pills, particularly since Eminem had already been through rehab and shouldn't have had them. They had a screaming argument about it.

During the fight, Kim told Marshall they weren't going to do the video with him after all. When the radio interviewer asked Kim if "*Mockingbird* was a bunch of a bull too?" Kim said, "That one and *When I'm Gone*, I listen to those songs, and I'm like 'Whatever.' Nothing like that is going on in the real world."

Pressed about whether she and Marshall were soul mates who would marry again, Kim said she couldn't stand him as a person anymore and that he made her "throw up" in her mouth every time she thought of him. She called him a horrible person.

Regarding this period of his life, Eminem actually seems to agree with her today. To *Rolling Stone,* he said "It creeps me out sometimes to think of the person I was. I was a terrible person. I was mean to people. I treated people around me shitty. Obviously, I was hiding something. I was fucked up inside, and people with those kinds of problems tend to put up this false bravado – let me attack everyone else, so the focus is off me. But of course, everybody knew. There were whispers, murmurs."

Eminem goes on to explain that no one dared to tell him he needed help because if anyone showed the slightest hint of thinking that he would blow his top. He says, "they would be gone," the implication being they would be fired or out of his life.

Asked by *Rolling Stone* if he could describe the day he almost died, he said

"I remember I got the methadone from somebody I'd

gone to looking for Vicodin. This person said, "These are just like Vicodin, and they're easier on your liver." I thought, "It looks like Vicodin, it's shaped like Vicodin – fuck it." I remember taking one in the car on the way home, and thinking, 'Oh, this is great.' Just that rush. I went through them in a couple of days, then went back and got more. But I got a lot more."

He goes on to say:" I got up to use the bathroom…I fell. I hit the floor hard. I got back up, tried again – and boom, I fell again. And that time I couldn't get up…All I remember was hitting the bathroom floor and waking up in the hospital."

Once again, it was nearing Christmas and Hailie's birthday when Eminem overdosed on drugs. This time by accident. It was December 2007.

Marshall told *Vibe* magazine, "Had I have got to the hospital about two hours later, I would have died. My organs were shutting down. My liver, kidneys, everything. They were gonna have to put me on dialysis. They didn't think I was gonna make it. My bottom was gonna be death."

CHAPTER FOUR

Mama had a baby and its head popped off
But mama don't want me the next thing I know I'm gettin' dropped off
Ring, ring, ring on the doorbell of the next-door neighbors on their front porch
But they didn't want me neither so they left me on someone else's lawn
'Til someone finally took me in my great aunt and uncle Edna and Charles
They were the ones who were left in charge

Family
(Ain't nothin' but a White Trash Party)

IN 2004, *ROLLING STONE* MAGAZINE ASKED EMINEM, "WHO in your family loved you?"

Eminem responded by talking about his Aunt Edna and Uncle Charles in Missouri.

"They were older, but they did things with me; they let me stay the weekends there, took me to school, bought me things, let me stay and watch TV, let me cut the grass to get five dollars, took me to the mall. Between them and my Uncle Ronnie, they were my solidity."

Asked if his father's relatives ever connected him with his father, Marshall said: "They'd tell me he was a good guy. But a lot of times he'd call, and I'd be there — maybe I'd be on the floor coloring or watching TV — and it wouldn't have been nothing for him to say, 'Hey put the kid on the phone.' He coulda talked to me."

ON THE OTHER side of his family, his mother's side was Eminem's, Uncle Ronnie. Many people already know that Ronnie killed himself from the song *Stan*

I read about your Uncle Ronnie too I'm sorry
I had a friend kill himself over some bitch who didn't
    want him

Ronnie was also mentioned in the song *Cleaning Out My Closet* with the painful lyric aimed at Debbie "Remember when Ronnie died, and you said you wished it was me? Well, guess what I am dead, dead to you as can be."

Debbie has admitted to the blurting out the comment one day after Kim had allegedly stolen her couch, and Marshall had allegedly hurled verbal abuse at her.

The two boys were born only six weeks apart, a late baby for his grandma Betty Kresin who lived in a trailer park in Warren, Michigan, a place that Eminem calls "the trailer park capital of the world."

About Ronnie, Marshall said, "He was just like my best friend. He was the only family that I had that I was close to." His grandmother said the boys hated to be separated from each other.

The famous lines in *Stan* refer to the circumstances of Ronnie's death.

But Debbie mentions in her book that Ronnie was kicked out of the US army because he couldn't stand guns. She claims this as evidence of her belief that Ronnie was murdered.

Debbie's secret "Heart and Soul" Twitter account was only exposed after she started railing at people who tweeted about her two brothers.

"My baby bro was shot at close range. Murdered! (Just like) with my brother Todd! To tell my family suicide……. you're totally wrong, don't talk about my brothers unless you have the facts. Thank you!"

No one else appears to agree with Debbie about this. Her twitter with its alt-right rants and delusional tweets about her family seems to give credence to Eminem's lines on *Headlights*

"Now, the medication is taking over and your mental state's deteriorating slow, and I'm way too old to cry this shit is painful, though."

Ronnie was Betty Kresin's (Eminem's grandmother) sixth child from her third marriage. Eminem remembers his uncle Ronnie buying the *'Breakin'* album in 1981.

> *"When I was 9 years old, my uncle put me on to the Breakin' soundtrack. The first rap song I ever heard was Ice-T, Reckless, I was fascinated."*

At this time, Eminem was actually lying about his age and experiences to all media because of his fear that he'd have to stop rapping at age 30 as he'd be too old.

Eminem was actually eleven and twelve at the time these songs came out. Of course, it makes more sense that an eleven-year-old or a twelves year old would get hooked on such music rather than a nine-year-old.

Marshall was too shocked to even attend Ronnie's funeral and just isolated himself, listening to Ronnie's tapes. When he asked his grandmother if he could use Ronnie's voice in a song, she became angry and threatened to sue.

Betty Kresin was furious with Marshall for not coming to the funeral and held several other grudges against her grandson.

> "I was kind of bitter about him writing about my dead son, because the last five years of my deceased boy's life, Marshall had not even seen him. Marshall – Eminem – and my son Ronnie were very close. He idolized Ronnie, and Ronnie loved him. He never even came to Ronnie's funeral, and he has never put the first flower on Ronnie's grave. He doesn't do anything – he won't go near the grave.
>
> The chain that Marshall wears around his neck, the dog-tag – that was Ronnie's. I gave him the dog-tag, he makes duplicates, he sells them now, and that really

> broke my heart, because this is something sacred to me that I gave the boy. If my son could speak to you today from the grave, he would say, "Marshall stop some of the garbage, makeup with your family, life's too short."

Kresin clearly didn't understand that the reproduction of the dog tag was probably done by merchandisers who quite possibly had Eminem sign off on a bunch of stuff he didn't even read through. In fact, Paul may well have done the signing off on such things for him. Never-the-less the fight between the two led to Eminem not using Ronnie's voice on any.

It is undeniable that teenage Marshall used to idealize Ronnie. Ronnie was the one who taught Emienm to rap, and for many years, they shared a great love of rapping.

But one day, Marshall told Ronnie about his dream to become a major rapper on the Detroit scene. Ronnie scoffed and told Marshall neither of them would ever make it as rappers, and that he had given up.

The story of Eminem's Uncle Ronnie is the ultimate story about why NOT to kill yourself. Imagine that your best friend in the whole world is your younger nephew. Imagine that you TAUGHT HIM HOW TO RAP. (Marshall was actually embarrassed sometimes because he thought his uncle Ronnie could rap better than he could!) Imagine that the two of you guys rap together all the time, but then he moves away from the area.

You grow apart. Your younger nephew comes to visit you and starts talking about the dreams of being a rapper you once shared...and you know what Ronnie did? He told his nephew he was into heavy metal now, that dreams of being a rapper were pipe dreams and that he'd given it all up.

Then you kill yourself over your poverty and your girlfriend dumping you.......5 years after your death your nephew Eminem signs to Dr. Dre! This is the sad story of Ronnie Dean Polkingharn, Eminem's uncle.

The story of Eminem's Uncle Todd, Debbie's other brother, is also shocking. Debbie tells a sickening tale of how one day, while heavily pregnant, she was standing talking to her brother Todd when a man called Mike Harris ran up to them. He allegedly grabbed Debbie, pulled up her top, held a knife to her stomach, and yelled, "I'll cut that baby out and hand it to you." Debbie said his eyes were red, and he was clearly on drugs.

Todd beat him off and chased him up the driveway. Debbie believes later problems with her pregnancy with Nathan were caused by the shock of this knife threat.

Mike Harris was Todd's brother in law and in Debbie's telling was some kind of psychopath who got off on threatening people with the worst things imaginable.

Debbie implies that Mike's sister Janice, Todd's wife, had an affair with her father, Bob Nelson. When Janice and Todd's second son was born, Janice named him after Eminem's grandfather, Bob.

The next horrific story about Mike Harris involves Eminem's, Uncle Todd.

One day when Todd and his wife, Janice, stopped to pick up some groceries, Todd sat in the car, minding little Bobby and his other baby son. Eminem's uncle had just come off a flight and had jetlag.

Suddenly Janice's brother Mike appeared pointing at Bobby and shouting, "I'm gonna rape the little bastard on the back seat!"

Todd started rummaging in the glove compartment for the spare keys to start the car. But instead, he found an antique pistol belonging to his wife. He waved it at Harris, who fled. A few minutes later, Harris reappeared in his car with a sawn-off shotgun and shouted: "I'm going to kill those kids."

Terrified Todd grabbed his wife's rusty 38 and began firing Harris, continued to make death threats, and attempted to karate kick the gun from his hands. Todd fired again; a bullet hit Harris in the back of his shoulder blade. Although Todd went to the police immediately and handed over the gun, ballistics experts concluded that Harris was attempting to run when Todd shot him.

Eminem's uncle was sentenced to eight years in prison for manslaughter. Todd studied law in prison and campaigned against asbestos use in prisons. But in the end, Debbie lost a second brother to suicide. Todd Nelson shot himself in the head.

The media has often claimed that the explanation for Todd's suicide was that he had become depressed over a neighboring sheriff's rottweiler, which was terrorizing his family. This is an odd story.

Also odd is the fact that Todd chose Marshall's birthday to shoot himself in the head. Was this another attempt by Todd to protest against Eminem's fame? Was Todd yet another person in Eminem's orbit who became depressed comparing his own life to the super star?

Debbie doesn't seem to think so. Eminem's mom firmly believes that both Ronnie and Todd were killed by someone in revenge for the death of Mark Harris. This is evidenced by her comments on Twitter.

Upon Todd's death, some journalists posted clickbait lies about this uncle having been a father figure to Eminem. In reality, he was no such thing. Todd was in prison much of

Marshall's youth, and he usually had nothing good to say about his famous nephew.

Todd berated Marshall in the press for insulting his sister. Todd is the one person who claims Eminem was lying about his mom for street cred and that Debbie never drank or took drugs.

There may be some truth *both* in Debbie's claims that "Marshall lived in an alcohol and drug-free home," and Marshall's repeated claims that his mother was a drug addict. The answer being that Debbie's problems were prescription drugs that she was legally entitled to possess.

In 1990 Debbie was rear-ended by a drunk driver and claims this ruined her life. According to Debbie, prior to this accident, she had worked as a cab driver, even owning three classic cars herself and her own small cab company. But her accident ended all that and led her to be the welfare mom Eminem complains so bitterly about.

Debbie does not name the medication she went on for panic attacks caused by the accident. But according to Eminem, it was valium which he himself later became addicted to.

His mother has said:

To me, drugs are illegal substances like cocaine and heroin, not something the doctor prescribes. Marshall's comments and lyrics really hurt.

However fellow Detroit MC Hush (Dan Carlisle), had this to say about Debbie's drug addiction:

"When Eminem got back from LA recording the Slim Shady LP, he picked up me and Bizarre (one of the rappers in

Eminem's group D12). He went to buy his little brother a PlayStation at *Best Buy*, then we went to his mother's place in the trailer park on 26 Mile. His mom tried to be nice, but she didn't look so good. I'd been forewarned by Em, but it was a bit of shock to see her so blew out.

But then the first thing Em does is lift up her mattress and look for pills. When he says, "Where do you think I picked up the habit?" on the Marshall Mathers LP, he means it."

My fuckin' bitch mom's suin' for 10 million
She must want a dollar for every pill I've been stealin'
Shit, where the fuck you think I picked up the habit?
All I had to do was go in her room and lift up her
    mattress

Debbie, in her book, denies ever keeping any of her medications under her mattress and somewhat laughably claims that her lawyer *forced* her to sue Eminem for ten million just to try and teach him to show her some respect.

"Big Naz" Williams Eminem's former bodyguard claims that during a tour while visiting Kansas, a lot of Eminem's relatives turned up to the tour bus, and they were all asking for money.

Williams tells of how he kicked all the groupies off the bus so that Eminem's drunken family members had room to get on and describes them as a cross between *The Beverly Hillbillies* and *South Park*.

The former bodyguard says Debbie was friendly and polite to him, but that she brought a photographer with her and then charged people $20 to take pictures with her son, and sold the photos to the local news for future stories.

Marshall begged the bodyguard not to let his mom near the stage as she would want to become part of the show.

According to Williams, the bodyguard Marshall did apparently reminisce with his relatives with some minor arguments for a while, before kicking them off, so he could get back to drugs and the hand-picked best-looking groupies.

Debbie, in her book, recalls the good times with her son. School-age Eminem mimed songs in front of his mirror and filled notebooks with poetry and drawings of superheroes. During the 80s, Marshall became a sidewalk breakdancer charging people five cents to see him breakdance.

But when Marshall was nineteen, he claims Debbie kicked him out of her house. Sending him to his grandmother's and keeping Nate with her.

Eminem's half-brother, Nathan, was removed from his mother's care by the state of Michigan at age ten years old. But the rhyme is everything in Hip Hop and to Eminem, so in the song *Headlights,* he pretends Nate was taken away at eight because it rhymes with Nate and state.

Eminem talks about it in an interview.

"I was 23. But when Nate was taken away, I always said if I ever get in a position to take him, I would take him. I tried to apply for full custody when I was twenty, but I didn't have the (financial) means. I couldn't support him. I watched him when he was in the foster home. He was so confused. I mean, I cried just goin' to see him at the foster home. The day he was taken away, I was the only one allowed to see him. They had come and got him out of school. He didn't know what the fuck was goin' on."

In her book, Debbie bizarrely explains that when they told

her, they'd decided she had Munchausen Syndrome by Proxy that she thought it must have something to do with dwarfism. Debbie said she was short, and Nathan's father was short, and Nathan was short for his age. Hilariously she relates it to The *Wizard of Oz* movie's Munchkins. She really believed that might have something to do with the diagnosis.

According to Debbie, Nathan was being beaten at school by bullies just like Marshall had been (although presumably not quite as badly), and this had caused his various injuries.

Eminem's mom also claims that Nathan tripped on a motel carpet while they were on holiday visiting relatives. She said he was rushed to hospital and treated for a concussion, but had memory lapses for years afterward. She also claims that Nathan is dyslexic and that after the accident teachers complained he'd stopped being able to read at all and blamed it on his mother.

Debbie claims that she had to nurse both her boys back to health after beatings from bullies

It is certainly proven that the beatings Marshall received in elementary school were severe. Marshall reportedly had to be retaught the simplest things, such as how to button his shirt and put on his shoes.

According to Debbie, this was the first time she quit working as a taxi driver and went on welfare to take care of her son. Marshall was nine years old.

After suffering this with her first child, Debbie says she became overprotective with Nathan. (Some of her family members have claimed she isolated Nathan and didn't let him play with other kids after school.)

Debbie's status as an unreliable narrator can perhaps be seen in the fact that she claims Nathan was made to wear a dunce cap in 1995, a practice that was supposedly abolished by American schools in the late 1950s.

Eminem's mom claims that the very first day she returned Nathan to school after his accident in the hotel that child protective services came to the school and placed Nathan in state custody.

The accusations against Debbie were that she had kept Nathan from going to school, that she hit him with a hairbrush and that she chased him out of the house for listening to rap music. Debbie denies all of this. Nathan had only just had his tenth birthday at the time, and according to Eminem, he was very confused about the whole situation.

The generational history of child abuse in Eminem's family has been confirmed by Marshall's grandma Betty Kresin who told reporters how she was raised by her own grandmother "When my grandmother wasn't switching me 'till I was black and blue she used to put me in a spooky closet full of mothballs and lock me in. Debbie was born on her birthday, and I feel she was under a curse."

Likewise, Debbie has to say about Better Kresin her own mother "I call her only my birth mother as giving birth is the only bit of mothering, she ever did for me. "

However, Eminem's complaints against his mother were most often for emotional and verbal abuse. Apart from the accusation that she sometimes gave him and Nathan valium to sedate them. Marshall has rarely accused her of being violent and has never accused her of hitting them. He did once call her "a quarterback with a hairbrush," which does suggest that a hairbrush was her weapon of choice if she ever did hit her kids. The inference from Eminem was that she *threw* hairbrushes.

Kim has confirmed this to *Mojo in the Morning,* telling them Debbie used to throw her hairbrush at Marshall. Social workers accused Debbie of hitting Nathan with her hairbrush.

Eminem, who was still unknown at the time, was subpoenaed by the prosecution in 1996. He refused to answer the question of whether he loved his mother but told the court that his mother was a "good mother" rather than a "bad mother" and that Debbie had only ever hit Nathan once giving him one spanking at age five.

Eminem's half-brother Nathan had a short-lived rap career, which he seems to have put aside in favor of being a part-time actor and full-time personal trainer. He is married to Ashley Mae, and the couple have three children.

Ashley Mae even gets a mention in Eminem's song *Arose* on his December 2017 album *Revival*.

> *And, little bro, keep making me proud*
> *You better marry that girl 'cause she's faithfully down*
> *And when you're exchanging those sacred vows*
> *Just know that if I could be there, I would*
> *And should you ever see parenthood, I know you'll be good at it*
> *Oh, almost forgot to do something, thank my father too*
> *I actually learned a lot from you*
> *You taught me what not to do*
> *And, Mom, wish I'd have had the chance*
> *To have one last heart-to-heart honest and open talk with you*

Eminem told *Rolling Stone* that the closest thing he ever had to a father figure, while he was growing up, was his half-brother Nathan's dad- Fred Samra.

However, this was only because Fred took Marshall on some fun outings, while having his visitation with Nathan, Samra still didn't play that big, or consistent a father figure in Nathan's life, and Debbie claims Fred Samra infuriated and hurt her by asking for his parental rights to Nathan to be severed to get out of child support.

Eventually, Nathan decided in 2018, that he'd take the name of the man who'd played the biggest father roll overall in his life, his big brother.

A judge at the Michigan court, where Nate filed the application, granted his wish to become Nathan Mathers. This should probably help Nathan's acting career along.

Eminem's last performance of Cleanin' Out My Closet was August 25, 2013, only a few months before the album, The Marshall Mathers LP2, and the song Headlights came out in November.

But in these later renditions, it seems Eminem would only perform the hook of this song and the first verse dealing with being hated by the public.

Then again, he did sometimes lead the crowd in a "Fuck you, Mom" chant before starting the first verse…giving credence to his uncle Todd's claims that Eminem was using people's resentments towards their own mothers to his advantage.

Eminem denies this even in the song itself. "I would never diss my own Mama just to get recognition.)

Later in the song, he says

But guess what? You're getting older now, and it's
    cold when you're lonely
And Nathan's growing up so quick he's gonna know
    that you're phony

Marshall's half-brother Nathan can be seen in a lot of Eminem's videos, famously in Stan, he plays "Mathew" Stan's brother.

Nate is also a musician, but he only has only six songs

released on iTunes. He used his middle name as his last name when recording these songs.

Ironically Nate Kane's most famous song might be Shadow of a Celebrity.

Nate was not the son of Marshall Mathers Jr Eminem's dad, but after being mistakenly called Nate Mathers by many people for years, he eventually changed his name by deed poll to Nate Kane Mathers.

Debbie Mather's secret Twitter account is @heartandsoul with some numbers after it. She sadly follows some obviously fake Twitter accounts of people pretending to be her relatives.

She follows a fake *Twitter* account of her granddaughter Hailie. Hailie's verified *Instagram* account plainly states that she has no *Twitter* account. However, the fake Hailie's Twitter reposts all of Hailie's *Instagram* photos, so at least Debbie gets to see those pictures.)

The fake Hailie does not follow Debbie back. Eminem's main account does not follow Debbie back.

Debbie frequently tweets to Nathan and sometimes tweets Paul Rosenberg demanding that he mail her a CD she claims he once promised to send her.

Debbie sadly trolls people such as Christine Blasey Ford, spewing misogynistic aggression at women she perceives as liberals.

She usually ends her insulting tweets to people like Obama, Hillary Clinton, and Christine Blasey with "Sad." In exact imitation of Trump's tweets.

Debbie flips from expressing rage towards liberals to talking about how the world needs more love, and how we should all show more love. But more than anything else, she spends time tweeting links to music videos that she calls "Golden Oldies."

Of Marshall's songs, *Not Afraid* is clearly her favorite, and she has described it as one of his best songs.

Debbie also frequently tweets links to Nathan's music and tweets praise to his real account, to which she seems to get no response.

She does seem to have a couple of older women who chat to her and call her Debbie, as well as some friendly tweets to her, from respectful Eminem fans who have caught on.

Reading Debbie's alt-right conspiracy tweets Eminem's *Headlights* lyrics: *"your mental state's deteriorating slow, and I'm way too old to cry this shit is painful, though."*

and *"I will always love you from afar cause you're my mom,"* seem a little less surprising.

While the press liked to claim that *Headlights* was "an apology to his mom," the song actually doubles down on former accusations. At most, it's an apology for songs as vicious as *Cleaning Out My Closet*, and *My Mom* but not a retraction of former allegations.

Instead, the song explains that he understands Debbie more now after his own drug problems. He offers forgiveness from himself and Nathan.

The song *Headlights* is not entirely forgiving, however. It still includes the lines, *"And I think of Nathan being placed in a home. And all the medicine you fed us. And how I just wanted you to taste your own."*

Eminem has also explained in interviews that he'd never realized that addiction could be hereditary and that his work on becoming sober and clean had helped him understand his mother's addiction to prescription pills a lot more and helped him reach a place of forgiveness. Given Debbie's tales of his father's alcoholism it seems Eminem may have inherited a gene for addiction from both sides of his family.

To *Rolling Stone* Marshall said: "You start getting

different perspectives on certain things. Lots of people go through lots of things and don't have this or don't have that in their lives — and I guess it's just what you do with it. Um, I will say this. I love her because she's my mom. I will always love her because of that."

In addition to following her family members and some fake accounts of her family members, Debbie also follows multiple accounts about elder abuse, and she follows President Trump. She sends Tweets to Obama telling him "go back to Kenya" (Yikes!), And even in 2019, Debbie still sends occasional tweets to Hillary Clinton telling her she is "a miserable person" "because of (her) emails."

As offensive as some of these tweets may be to many people, it's important to remember that Debbie Mathers is in her sixties, possibly still suffering from cancer, and should be left in peace.

CHAPTER FIVE

I built this castle
Now we are trapped on the throne
I'm sorry we're alone
I wrote my chapter
You'll turn the page when I'm gone
I hope you'll sing along
This is your song

———

Eminem's Children and his Luxurious Lifestyle
   (*Straighten Up, Little Soldier.*)

"WITHOUT HAILIE, THERE IS NO EMINEM. I KNOW THAT sounds bananas, but the definition of focus is direct attention, and he gives direct attention to Hailie. That's all that matters." – *Proof to Vanity Fair Magazine.*

The year Marshall's brother Nathan spent in foster care had a significant impact on young Eminem. Marshall spent

1996 desperate to get custody of his younger brother and get him out of care.

Marshall was allowed to visit his ten-year-old brother in foster care and found him in a confused and miserable state. Poor Nathan had even reportedly suffered several physical injuries from being beaten up by other foster kids.

But with Marshall's on again off again work history (he was frequently fired then rehired from fast food joints) and his low wages as a short-order cook, the authorities refused to allow him to adopt Nathan.

However, in November of 1996, after accepting a plea deal Debbie herself was finally able to get Nathan out of foster care

But Nathan complained to *Face* magazine in 2002 that his mother was crazy. Once Nathan was sixteen, Marshall was able to formally adopt him. This makes Nathan technically Eminem's oldest child and heir.

Debbie claims Nathan wanted to live with Marshall, so Debbie let him. Eminem and Nathan claim that Debbie rang Marshall and screamed at him to take Nathan, or she would put him back in foster care. This may have been a one-off moment of rage for Debbie that cost her dearly.

More background on why Eminem adopted Nathan comes from Kim to *Mojo in the Morning*. Kim admitted her own past problems with cocaine and alcohol addictions. But she said her addictions made her act very different from the way Debbie acted because of her prescription pill addiction.

In another radio interview prior to the release of 8 Mile to cinemas, Kim said: "Marshall's mother is the worst person in the world I can't believe they got someone so beautiful (Kim Basinger) to play her."

Rumors were that Nathan and Marshall would perform a

skit for friends imitating Debbie. "Goddammit, I know someone's been in my purse. Nathan, it was you wasn't it get out of my fucking house. Where are you going? If you leave this house, your grounded you little mother fucker." This makes one recall the lyrics of the 2002 song *Cleaning Out My Closet*.

> *But put yourself in my position, just try to envision*
> *Witnessin' your mama poppin' prescription pills in the kitchen*
> *Bitchin' that someone's always goin' through her purse and shit's missin'*

Even Proof backed the claims that Debbie would frequently start screaming and then throw a teenage Marshall out of the house, due to the effect her prescription drugs had on her. DeShaun has said, "Shoot, I was at her house more than Marshall was."

Marshall would even do a quick skit of his mother doing this, during the *Up in Smoke Tour*, before performing the song *Kill You*.

All of this led Marshall to adopt Nathan in 2002.

But Nathan stayed in touch with his mom, and it was Nathan who suggested Eminem pay for Debbie's breast cancer treatment and write an apology of some sorts to their sick mother, leading to the song *Headlights* released in 2014. Sadly, however, since Nathan doesn't seem to ever respond to his mother's tweets praising him, they may have fallen out once again.

When Eminem decided to foot the bill for Debbie's medical care, it was the first thing that he had paid for, for her, since she attempted to sue him for ten million dollars.

So, Nathan is Eminem's oldest child by adoption and is likely in line to inherit a portion of his wealth. For both his sixteen and seventeenth birthdays, Marshall brought his brother/son a brand-new sports car.

The younger children were driven to school in Eminem's expensive cars, such as his Cadillac Escalade. Eminem owns twelve cars at this present time. He also owns a huge Hummer H2 to fit all his friends and family a classic, a convertible, 1999 Mustang GT convertible in honor of the year his first well-known album blew up. In addition, Marshall owns a Ferrari 599 GTO, a Ferrari 430 Scuderia, and his Audi R8 Spyder. Also, an Aston Martin V8 Vantage, a Porsche Carrera GT, and a McLaren MP4-12C and a Chrysler 300c.

Eminem's next oldest child is his niece by marriage and adopted daughter Alaina Marie Scott Mathers, who was born on May 3, 1993.

Biologically, Alaina is the daughter of Dawn Scott, Kimberly Mather's twin sister, who died of a drug overdose. Marshall and Eminem adopted Alaina long before Dawn died because of Dawn's drug problems. Alaina has a twin herself, a disabled brother named Adam, who was put in the custody of his biological father and has not been adopted by Eminem.

Eminem and Kim often babysat Alaina, and she was Hailie's childhood friend. Eminem became fed up with watching the little girl being bounced from rental property to rental property and wanted to fix things for her before he had the money to do so.

Alaina was originally named Amanda Marie Scott by her mother Dawn, but when Dawn drug abuse and legal troubles became too much, Kim and Marshall adopted the baby girl together and changed her name to Alaina. She is referred to as Lainey in the song *Mocking Bird*.

Alaina Mathers studied public relations at the University of Oakland, a public university in Rochester Hills, Michigan. She may be working now as a public relations consultant.

In 1999 Alaina's birth mother, Dawn had another son name Patrick often called PJ. Sadly, the courts removed Patrick from his mother's care because of her drug use and gave Kim's mother Kathleen Sluck and Kim, joint custody of Patrick. Dawn was Kim's fraternal twin sister.

Dawn's boyfriend Les Martin, whom she had lived with on and off for four years, also gave an interview to Radar. Les said, "Dawn was doing any kind of drugs she could get her hands on. Heroin, cocaine, Adderall. If it was a pill, she would take it. But Klonopin was her real downfall. She was swallowing them things like candy."

Les claimed that he had called Kim many times and asked her to help her sister. He said: "I've been trying like hell to save her life. I've had numerous conversations with Kim about trying to get her help, and it just wasn't a conversation she wanted to have. She wanted to let Dawn go. I was so frustrated."

He said Dawn had been sleeping on couches and even on the street.

Dawn Scott chose to do a shocking interview with celebrity news outlet *Radar* telling them that she was a homeless woman.

> "I have a millionaire brother-in-law and a sister with money up the ass, but they're refusing to give me any help. It's a betrayal. He's been part of our family since he was fifteen!"

However, even former friends of Kim's, who now claim to dislike her, admit that while Dawn was on welfare, Kim would always pay all her utility bills.

But Kim feared that the money she was giving Dawn to keep the power on in her flat for her and PJ, may have been spent on drugs instead. Eventually, joint custody of PJ was also given to Kathleen Sluck and Kim.

Former friends of Dawn claimed that because of her drug addictions, Dawn had several abortions before getting her tubes tied. But she had a particular fondness for little PJ and would kidnap him from Kathleen Sluck's property to have him back.

Dawn spent her rent money on drugs and ended up living rough on the street. Finally, she turned up at her sister's mansion and demanded they give her five thousand dollars or a mobile home to live in, or she would go to the tabloids and expose all their worst secrets.

They bought Dawn the mobile home, and Kim did not speak to her sister for weeks but eventually calmed down, and their relationship was back to normal.

However, Dawn did eventually go to the tabloids anyway and also alleged.

"Marshall hit my sister on-and-off. One time he did it in front of me, and I started choking him. He called his security, but they refused to intervene."

In Eminem's 2017 *Revival* track *Bad Husband* Eminem seems to admit the first allegation.

> *"Cause it was such a dumbass excuse. You hit me once and that I would use. To continue the pattern of abuse Why did I punch back? Girls, your dad is a scumbag. I'm confused."*

Yes, sadly, Eminem appears to be admitting to being a wife beater on *Revival*, even if the admins at Genius.com won't tolerate such an annotation on *Bad Husband*. (Eminem is an investor with *Genius*.)

Dawn also alleged

> "Three days after they remarried, Kim went over to their other house to surprise him. But Kim's the one who got surprised because Marshall was fooling around with his life coach! One night I called my sister and told her I had nowhere to go. (was homeless) She said, 'That's not my problem. Don't bother me,' and hung up."

Just four months after Dawn gave this interview, her body was discovered in her Detroit trailer park home after her death from an apparent heroin overdose. She died in the trailer Kim and Eminem had bought her.

At her funeral, Kim said "Dawn was my sweet, beautiful sister who lost her way,"

On the funeral home's website, where loved ones are invited to leave a message for the deceased Kim wrote,

"I kept a light lit for her, hoping she'd find her way back to me. I miss her and love her more than anything I could ever say. I wish she was here so I could hug her and tell her I love her.

Half of me is gone, and I will never feel whole again," Mathers continued. "She made me laugh and kept me on my toes.

She was the best sister and friend in the world, and I will miss her until we are together again."

As sad and tragic as Dawn's death is one blessing seems to be that all her children are well cared for. Adam Scott, who is disabled lives with his father. Patrick (PJ) Scott is well cared for by his aunt Kim who adopted him and Kim's net worth is currently two million, so she certainly has the financial resources to care for him. And Alaina was cared for by Eminem, who had full custody of her since Kim's prison stint.

Today Alaina Mathers has a Bachelor's degree in Public Relations from the University of Oakland, a top-rated academic institution in southeast Michigan.

Tales from acquaintances of how Eminem interacted with his two older children in the early days are fun.

Former babysitters of Hailie's said he enjoyed entertaining his daughters with imitations and was apparently particularly good at Kermit, the frog.

He would sometimes forgo the studio to jump on the trampoline with Hailie and Alaina or play barbie dolls with them. He later did the same with Whitney.

A former friend of Kim's claimed that Hailie would be

allowed all the Mountain Dew and candy she wanted at 12:30 a.m. if she demanded it and that babysitters or Eminem would all drive-thru *Taco Bell* for dinner almost every single day because it was what Hailie asked for.

While Hailie and Alaina were still little, Eminem had a movie theater built into the basement of his Clinton Township home in Macomb County. The movie theatre had curtains that opened as the lights dimmed, fiber optics on the ceiling that gave the appearance of stars, and all the seats were recliners. The home cinema had a popcorn popper, a soda fountain, and a nacho dispenser. Eminem had a game room with 8 arcade games, a jukebox, a pool table, and air hockey. The pièce de résistance was a giant Spiderman statue. Eminem also had many *Spiderman* comics and other marvel superhero comics around the house, a childhood passion that never died.

Eminem told *Rolling Stone* in 2002, "When I'm home, I wake her up in the morning, I feed her some cereal, watch a little TV, take her to school and pick her up. Lately, I've been taking her to the studio, because that's where I spend most of my time. She has fun there, there's video games for her and stuff. Coloring books and crayons — thank God for those. We watch a lot of movies, just typical shit. She's really into *The Powerpuff Girls* and *Hey Arnold!* and *Dora the Explorer* — ever seen that one? It's the same episode all week long because it teaches kids numbers and how to speak Spanish. By Friday, you know it by heart. I watch that with her, then I go listen to my songs over and over.

Eminem's recording studio is equally full of fun for his kids and himself. It, too, has a popcorn machine, comic books, and Mexican Lucha libre wrestling masks on the walls. A large painting of Biggie and 2Pac graces one wall, while a plaque leaning against another celebrates Eminem's status as SoundScan's Artist of the Decade: 32 million albums sold in 10 years a number larger than *The Beatles*.

He has a diet coke soda fountain in the lobby and drinks cup after cup every day. He's a self-described chain-drinker replacing former addictions with the fountain. To *Rolling Stone* magazine, he said, "There's aspartame in the cans," he says. "They say it's been known to cause cancer, so I cut that shit out. There's no aspartame in the fountain." He encourages his kids not to drink from cans either.

Also, in the studio for him and his kids to enjoy, there is a video arcade. Eminem loves vintage games.

According to *Rolling Stone,* Marshall's studio lobby is filled with arcade classics: Space Invaders, Donkey Kong, Frogger.

Eminem has an ambition to beat Steve Wiebe, who captured the world Donkey Kong record. (Two of Eminem's machines are autographed by Wiebe.) Eminem became interested in beating the score after watching a documentary about Wiebe.

Eminem has reported his own Donkey Kong score (465,800), which at the time was within the top 30 worldwide, though with increasing competition this score would now sit outside the top 100. The original high score was 872,000. This is now higher.

In his arcade, he also has Zelda games. The kids enjoyed the arcade, too, and Whitney occasionally still does.

Eminem's youngest child is Whitney Scott Mathers, born on April 16, 2002. After Kim and Eminem divorced the first time in 2001. Kim became involved with a Tattoo artist Eric Hartter. It is alleged that Eric Hartter was on the run from a drug conviction while Kim was giving birth to Whitney. As Eminem and Kim began a reconciliation process, Eminem adopted Whitney.

At first, Marshall talks about being very upset at the thought of Kim having a baby with another man. It was 2001 Marshall didn't know if they would ever be able to get back together, or if he could get his head around Kim being pregnant to another man. Eminem was worried about how the pregnancy would affect Hailie. Ultimately, he adopted the baby Whitney because Kim, after being sentenced to home detention, had cut off her tether and gone on the run from the law leaving the baby with Marshall. As a result, Kim spent February to October 2004 in prison.

The result was that Eminem gained full custody of all the children except Dawn's son Patrick (PJ), who went into the full care of his grandmother Kathleen Sluck.

After Kim came out of prison, she sued for custody of Hailie and got joint custody back. Perhaps thinking that the cost of fighting for just one child would at least connect her back with her family. Hence the strange situation where Eminem technically had full custody of Alaina and Whitney, but joint custody of Hailie. Of course, all this happened long before Parker Scott was born in 2013. According to a member of D12 who wanted to remain nameless, Parker is the only other child that Marshall shares joint custody of with Kim.

All three of Eminem's daughters must endure media and public scrutiny, but Hailie, his biological child, and the one child mentioned the most in his songs has arguably had it the worst.

An interesting comment on a Daily Mail article that included a picture of Hailee, with the caption "Hailee Scott seen at a drive-thru ATM last week" and a photo of her in her car- the comment underneath says ""Hailee Scott, seen at a drive-thru ATM last week" – "Wait, what??? WHO takes these pictures?? And WHY? And how is that even legal? I find that so highly disturbing."

Of course, it is legal as long as the pictures are taken outside in public, and they are taken by people desperate to make money from them. The commenter is right however that it is disturbing and it reminds one of the lyrics to Eminem's song *Castle* on his 2017 album *Revival* which has lyrics such as

> "I built this castle; now, we are trapped on the throne.
> I'm sorry we're alone,"

A song dedicated to Hailie, who cannot even stay in the car to use the ATM without being photographed.

The song goes on to say

I wrote my chapter
You'll turn the page when I'm gone
I hope you'll sing along
This is your song

Eminem told *NME* magazine in 2002:

> "When she grows up. She's gonna be able to go to college and be something I wasn't. If she never makes anything of herself, God forbid – I want her to do something, be a model, make music, be a doctor, anything – I'm gonna have that money there for her. It's about her now. We're here to reproduce. And I reproduced. So now my life is for her."

Hailie's name is "Hailie Scott" not for "privacy," as the

press sometimes claims but because Eminem and Kim were not married when Hailie was born. Her name has always been Scott.

Hailie graduated from Michigan State University with a Bachelor of Arts in Psychology in a very rare interview she told the press she was unsure what she wanted to do with it.

Although hundreds of fake Twitter accounts have been made in her name, Hailie has no Twitter account. As soon as she went on Instagram, she told *The Daily Mail,* "People have been reaching out through Instagram, as I don't have any management."

Hailie went on in this early interview to say that many companies had offered to collaborate with her since she had joined Instagram. She told *W* magazine that she was drawn to the "beauty world" 'and might be a good fit for cosmetics companies.

Hailie now makes a living for herself as an Instagram influencer. Companies that she may have a working relationship appear to include *Fenty Beauty by Rihanna, Maybelline, M·A·C Cosmetics, Puma, Forever21, Nike Women, Stella McCartney, Balmain,* and surprisingly even *Versace* despite her father's long-ago bad taste lyrics that he included just to wind up those who'd accused him in the past of homophobia.

Hey, it's me, Versace! Whoops, somebody shot me!
And I was just checkin' the mail
Get it? Checkin' the male?

Anyone who gets too upset over these lyrics should refer to the beginning of the song.

A lot of people ask me stupid fuckin' questions

A lot of people think that what I say on a record
Or what I talk about on a record
That I actually do in real life or that I believe in it
Or if I say that I wanna kill somebody
That I'm actually gonna do it or that I believe in it
Well, shit, if you believe that, then I'll kill you

Hailie also appears to advertise for Crush Footwear. Her name on Instagram is hailiejade.

Hailie is social media buddies with Rhianna, Beyoncé, Jessie Reyez, Shawn Mendes, and Ellen DeGeneres.

Both Hailie and Eminem have a close friendship with Ellen.

Eminem gave Ellen a warm birthday greeting on video in which he said, "Ellen! It's Marshall here. I wanted to tell you that I feel like I kind of knew you before we met. And now that we've met, I kind of feel like we're besties. So uh um I was probably going to move in. I'll…I'll talk to you about that later. I just wanted to say happy birthday I wanted to wish you a happy sixtieth birthday, you don't look a day over 20. I love you. The world loves you. We all love you. Happy birthday."

Hailie has a boyfriend that she met at Michigan State University named Evan McClintock. Evan majored in economics and is a keen golfer. They have been in a relationship for more than three years.

On the 19th of January 2016, Hailie's aunt Dawn Scott obituary read, "Dawn Scott is remembered as the "loving mother of Alaina, Adam, and Patrick. Cherished sister of Kimberly Mathers. Beloved daughter of Casimer and Kathleen Sluck. Dear Aunt of Whitney Scott, Hailie Scott, and Parker Scott. Dawn is survived by many extended loved ones and friends."

Kim was raising Alaina, Hailie, Whitney, and PJ until 2013 when she had her third biological child. This was her fifth child if you include the two children she adopted.

This fifth child's name is Parker Scott, whom Eminem is rumored to have adopted in 2013 presumably so the half-siblings could all be connected.

The only children mentioned that Eminem seems not to have adopted are Alaina's brother Patrick who lives exclusively with Kim. And Adam, Alaina's twin.

It is possible, however, that there is so much secrecy protecting little Parker because he is Eminem's own child. Kim and Marshall, having learned their lessons with their older children and working to shield this much younger child from the world, although a few pictures of Parker can be found online.

In 2013 Kim's mother, Kathleen Sluck, ran to the press to them that Kim and Marshall had reconciled and were getting along better than they ever had, both clean and really making something of their lives. Sluck revealed to the press that Eminem was building a custom-made house for Kim and was so excited about it. The couple later denied these rumors that they were getting back together and told the press that they were only friends, but this has led to speculation whether Parker might be Eminem's secret child. This is only a theory, however. A D12 member who wanted to remain anonymous claimed that Eminem adopted Parker in 2013. Kim told Mojo in the morning that her youngest child had autism and that she was struggling to come to terms with the extra parenting skills it takes to raise a special needs child.

Men over 35 are three times more likely to have a child with autism than younger men. Eminem was 41 when Parker was born. Did the two conspire to never make their adorable son's life as crazy as it has been for their three older daughters who cannot go out without being snapped by paparazzi? Parker is eighteen years younger than his sister Hailie? Are they doing this right the second time?

Fathers with ADHD and fathers with Asperger's are also quite likely to have an autistic child. The only distinction between the condition Asperger's and the condition named autism is that people with Asperger's did not have a speech delay as little children and learned to talk during the expected age range while people with other forms of autism all had at least a speech delay if they learned to speak at all. The diagnosis of Asperger's was dropped from the DSM V and replaced with Autism Spectrum Disorder covering all types of Autism, including those who never suffered a speech delay, previously called Asperger's.

Eminem has claimed to have Asperger's in three of his songs Legacy, Wicked Ways, and Heat.

> *I used to be the type of kid*
> *That would always think the sky is fallin'*
> *Why am I so differently wired? Am I a Martian?*
> *What kind of twisted experiment am I involved in?*
> *'Cause I don't belong in this world*
> *That's why I'm scoffin' at authority, defiant often*
> *Flyin' off at the handle at my mom*
> *No dad, so I am noncompliant at home*
> *At school, I'm just shy and awkward*
> *And I don't need no goddamn psychologist*
> *Tryna diagnose why I have all these underlyin'*
>   *problems*

It seems somewhat doubtful, however, that Eminem truly has diagnosable Asperger's. However, the famous singer

Suzanne Boyle has told how she was professionally diagnosed with the condition, so very successful musicians can certainly have Asperger's.

Suzanne Boyle, however, has shown real impairments, for example, showing such extreme distress in airports that she caused a public disturbance.

Another example is the story reported in UK tabloid newspaper *The Daily Express* regarding how famous millionaire Susan Boyle attempted to apply for a £6 an hour job in her local betting shop because it was something she'd always wanted to do. This shows a real lack of social awareness on a level that Eminem has never shown.

Eminem has actively tried to offend people as a marketing tool. A co-worker at *Gilbert Lodge* said that she told him writing a song about killing the mother of his child was sick. He responded, "Yeah, but it will make me a big one day." So that makes it hard to pinpoint any of Eminem's offensive behavior to a neurologically-based lack of social awareness.

Eminem's mom claimed Marshall had ADHD, however, which is genetically linked to autism and is a condition generally considered a less severe impairment than autism.

Another reason to doubt that Eminem has Asperger's is that it is possible Eminem just enjoys the way the word sounds and likes to rhyme things with it.

However, all that being said, it has become common in these modern times for people who feel less than socially adept to wonder if they have the condition, and Eminem is a workaholic who seems to live more of a hermit type lifestyle than a lot of other celebrities. However, a disorder is not considered a disorder unless diagnosed by a professional and proven to have a significant adverse effect on a person's life.

In an interview given to the *Rolling Stone Magazine*,

Marshall said, "In Court, I had to testify against (my mom). Nate, who was 9 at this time, was too scared to testify against his mom. His mom made him believe he was a hyperactive kid and that he was suffering from Attention Deficit Disorder. My mother said I was a hyper kid, and I wasn't, he said. She put me on Ritalin."

A mother thinking her child has ADHD is far from Munchausen's Syndrome by Proxy, and Eminem would have needed a diagnosis to get a prescription for Ritalin as would have Nathan. Munchausen's Syndrome by Proxy is a condition in which a mother actually harms her child so as to make the child appear to have a physical illness that the child does not. One appalling but classic example of true Munchausen's Syndrome by Proxy is Lacey Spears, who fed her son, Garnett, large amounts of salt through a gastrointestinal feeding tube, causing brain swelling, seizures, and death. Her motivation was apparently the attention she got on Facebook by talking about having a "sickly son." Garnett tragically died at age five, in 2014. Spears was convicted of second-degree murder and first-degree manslaughter in 2015.

Now, this is a very far cry from a mother who takes her son to the doctor, thinking he may have ADHD. ADHD is an authentic condition; however, the diagnosis is somewhat subjective as a diagnosis can only be made from a history of a child's behavior and tests that measure the ability to consistently concentrate on a task.

It is also somewhat unclear from various sources and court documents if Debbie was diagnosed by a doctor or if a social worker from child protective services simply decided she had the condition. Some sources say the "diagnosis" came from a social worker, but a social worker does not have the qualifications to make such a diagnosis. Debbie does claim, however, that the prosecution in the case of abuse against Nathan said she had Munchausen's Syndrome by Proxy. *If* this diagnosis presented in court was done by a social worker and not a doctor than Debbie was done a grave injustice.

Many fans of Eminem believe Debbie put Valium in his food because of the son *My Mom,* but the song is clearly exaggerated and farcical.

However, the moment in the song when Debbie asks Marshall to take some Valium so that he won't wake up, his brother appears to be more authentic. Eminem implies his mother drugged up herself sometimes drugged them to try to get them.

Since Nathan, Alaina, and Hailie are all adults now, the only child that Eminem is still definitely raising is Whitney, who is seventeen and in high school.

Eminem may or may not also be raising Parker who may or may not be his son, depending on whether the rumors of adoption from a D12 member are true or whether the rumors that Kim has another long-term secret relationship with a man who is Parker's biological dad are true.

Poor Whitney recently had to endure the media making a big production about her bio father again in 2019 when Eric Hartter pleaded guilty to being a prisoner possessing contraband as a fourth-time offender.

Radar Online reported that Hartter (Kim's former boyfriend and biological father of Whitney) first ran into legal trouble in December 2018 after he and two accomplices were arrested for allegedly stealing about $200 worth of Red Bull from a CVS.

Macomb Daily reported that a warrant was issued recently for the biological father of Eminem's adopted daughter after he failed to show up for his sentencing in another drug case. Hartter pleaded guilty in 2012 in Macomb Circuit Court to possession of a firearm by a felon and reckless use of a firearm for a Clinton Township incident and was sentenced to one year in jail, records say.

Macomb Daily also reported that in 2007, he pleaded guilty to possession of fewer than 25 grams of a controlled substance in Roseville. Hartter was convicted by a plea of receiving more than $100 in stolen property and breaking and entering a vehicle with intent to steal more than $5 in goods in Warren in 1999. Hartter was also held in contempt of court in January in a separate domestic case for failure to pay child support, ordered to serve 30 days or pay $1,000, court records say.

Radar Online also reported that while in jail, Hartter was arrested a second time for felony contraband, involving Fentanyl.

All of which explains why when Kim Mathers was on the run from the law, and then in prison, Eminem ended up adopting her child to another man.

After watching Nathan's misery in foster care, Marshall didn't want to consign Hailie's sister to foster care though, at one point, he considered never letting the two children see each other as he felt so messed up about Kim having a child to another man. Maturity, empathy, and compassion won out, and Eminem adopted the little girl that he no doubt loves a great deal.

Whitney's *Instagram* is whitneyscott8. She has posted the following on *Instagram*. "Happy National Coming Out Day! I am bisexual 💚 I would like to say you're perfect the way you are and that love is love! Be yourself!"

This is also interesting considering all the rumors from people like Eminem's Uncle Todd and from Hailie's babysitters about Kim being bisexual.

By 2019 Eminem's children, his brother Nathan that he

adopted, his niece Alaina that he adopted, and his daughter Hailie have all grown up, and the one child he is definitely still raising is Whitney. The other child that he may be partially helping Kim raise is little Parker. There is no doubt he loves all his children very much.

CHAPTER SIX

I still love your mother, that'll never change
Think about her every day, we just could never get it
  together, hey.
Wish there was a better way for me to say it
But I swear on everything, I'd do anything for her on
  any day

Love
(Spell it backwards. I'll show you.)

BOTH THE MEDIA AND PEOPLE ON SOCIAL MEDIA HAVE LINKED Eminem to the names of a great many women in attempts at clickbait, so it took some real in-depth research to find out the truth about Eminem's love life.

The following is an analysis of what has really happened in Eminem's love life, including which relationships actually happened and which were just click-bait that never happened.

Eminem and Mariah Carey- Status Real Relationship

In a *Vanity Fair* magazine interview, Eminem discussed his love life and his struggles with Kim. He talked about how hard it was to trust any new women for fear they were only interested in his fame and money.

Eminem was asked by the interviewer, "Why don't you try dating other celebrities who would understand you?" Eminem responded, "You know, I tried that, but I found that they were even crazier than I was."

The two celebrities he's referring to would be Mariah Carey and Britney Murphy confirmed but also possibly Tara Reid.

Eminem opened up about his relationship with Mariah Carey, during an interview on his *Sirius* Satellite Radio station, *Shade 45*.

"Yes, me and Mariah did have a relationship for about a good six, seven months," said Eminem. "(But) it didn't work. I wasn't really into what she was into; our personalities collided. She's a diva, and I'm a little more regular, I guess."

Mariah Carey always denied their relationship completely, while Eminem insisted that the relationship occurred.

In April 2018, Mariah Carey told *People* magazine that she had been battling bipolar disorder and revealed a 2001 diagnosis dated around the time of her breakup with Luis, and her admission gives some credence to the stories of how everything went down between Mariah and Eminem. Ultimately according to Eminem's friends, it was Marshall who broke off the relationship because Mariah was scaring and disturbing him with strange behavior.

The story begins in1999. Eminem met Mariah at an

awards show, but at the time, she was dating Luis Miguel, a singer, and Latin American icon. They broke up in 2001. And Eminem had just married Kim for the first time.

This was around the time she appears to have begun perusing Marshall, although, with Eminem's usual paranoia, he accuses her of sleeping with both him and Miguel at the same time in his 2009 song *The Warning*.

> *Call my bluff, and I'll release every fucking thing I got*
> *Including the voicemails right before you flipped*
>   *your top*
> *When me and Luis were tryin' to stick two CD's in the*
>   *same slot*

Friends say of Eminem that after that awards show Marshall would stop and stare at the TV whenever Mariah appeared on it and would read any of the magazines his aunt Betti Renee bought that had Mariah on the cover. A babysitter of Hailie's even claims that Eminem told her he had fantasied about Mariah Carey for years before becoming famous and was thrilled to now be "on her level."

Eminem was working on the *D12* 2001 album *Devil's Night* when Mariah's people got in contact with him, asking if he would collaborate with her on a song for a future album *Charmbracelet*, or if he would appear in one of her music videos.

Marshall agreed to meet with her, but Debbie Mathers claims something went wrong, and Mariah and her people were left waiting on the tarmac for four hours before Marshall's people came to take Mariah to Eminem's mansion.

At that first meeting, Mariah reportedly refused all the food offered to her, and would only drink wine. (Something

Eminem made fun of much later in his 2009 song *Bagpipes from Baghdad*.)

Marshall ultimately declined to be on her album.

At this stage in his career, Eminem was dissing pop stars and rejecting collaborations with pop artists. Something hard-core hip-hop fans admired. Later some hard-core hip hops fans would bemoan the fact he chose to work with pop stars on later albums starting with Recovery.

Marshall had it seemed only agreed to meet with Mariah because of his sexual and romantic crush on her. She appeared to reciprocate interest.

It was rumored that Luis Miguel had dumped Mariah because she wanted to have children. Now Mariah began sending numerous gifts to Hailie. A former baby sitter claims a toaster arrived that would burn the face of Hello Kitty into bread. Followed by more and more Hello Kitty merchandise, a pink Hello Kitty comforter set, Hello Kitty towels, a Hello Kitty print for Hailie's bedroom wall, Hello Kitty soap, bath gel, and bath mat for Hailie's bathroom suite,

Eventually, Hailie's bathroom and bedroom were completely full of Mariah's favorite cartoon character.

Mariah sent a life-size cut out of herself to decorate Hailie's room along with posters. At the time, Marshall was still enamored with Mariah and reportedly thought the gifts were very sweet.

At the time, Marshall and Kim had not yet adopted Alaina, although she was a frequent visitor to Eminem's home, arriving to play with her cousin Hailie or staying for long periods of time when her mother could not cope. But Mariah's focus was on Hailie as she was not aware of the importance of her little cousin to the superstar.

Mariah was soon flying her private helicopter out to see Eminem regularly.

Marshall, in turn, would bring his Aunt Betti Renee and Uncle Jack (that he had hired to help with housework), and he would fly them and their three kids out to New York to stay in Mariah's third-floor apartment in New York.

Soon, however, Marshall began to complain to his closest friends that he never saw Mariah eat and that he only saw her drink wine. He reportedly even told her once that she was an alcoholic, and she responded by pouring the bottle of wine she'd been drinking down the kitchen sink.

Marshall's biggest complaint, though, was the phone messages. Marshall complained to Hailie's baby sitter and friends that Mariah had blown off a weekend where he and Hailie were supposed to meet her in Florida but was calling him continually saying strange things that didn't make sense and leaving weird messages on his answer machine.

In 2001, Mariah became paranoid and would ring Marshall saying that her ex-boyfriend music executive, Tommy Mottola, had bugged both her phone and Marshall's.

Mariah began leaving Marshall messages saying Mottola was going to kill her. She also allegedly left phone messages saying aliens and UFOs were coming after her. One day Carey left Eminem a message saying that the police had come around to arrest her and cut her with a knife. It later turned out she had cut herself with a broken plate.

Mariah Carey would swing wildly from talking about aliens to saying she wanted to announce to the world that she and Eminem were in love.

It was around this time that Eminem changed his phone number, his cell phone number, and the phone number of his aunt Betti Renee who was at the time his live-in maid.

On *Mojo in the Morning* Hailie's babysitter, Jenny Watkins and Kim agreed that Jenny and Kim had been very close friends for a long time and babysat each other's kids often. But Jenny and Kim reportedly fell out after Jenny had a one-night stand with Marshall and according to Kim, tried to leave her husband for Eminem. Something which Marshall also confirmed in a separate interview with *Mojo in the Morning*.

Jenny and Kim had been so close as children that they even pretended they were cousins. The two women called each other cousin even into adulthood. But although Eminem and Kim were separated at that time, Kim became so angry about the one-night-stand that she insisted Marshall break off all contact with the unpaid babysitter.

Kim also claimed to Detroit's *Mojo in the Morning* radio show that Jenny was a swinger who had tried to get Kim to have a threesome with her and her husband.

The wild stories told by Marshall's friends about Mariah's bizarre answer phone messages seem more likely to be accurate, after Mariah's own admission of a diagnosis of bipolar disorder and a manic episode in 2001 that was so serious that she landed in the hospital. This was the very same year, Eminem claimed to have had a relationship with her.

The paranoid delusional answer machine messages on Marshall's phone about aliens and UFOs and murderous stalkers would indicate that Mariah Carey was experiencing psychosis a possible symptom of both bipolar 1 and less frequently of bipolar 2.

In her 2018 interview with *People* magazine, Mariah explained that she was hospitalized. She told *People* editor-in-chief, Jess Cagle, that for a long time, she thought she just had a severe sleep disorder.

"But it wasn't normal insomnia, and I wasn't lying

> awake counting sheep. I was working and working and working ... I was irritable and in constant fear of letting people down. It turns out that I was experiencing a form of mania."

Carey also revealed that for sixteen years, the years between 2001 and 2017, she was in denial.

Mariah, speaking to People magazine about the year 2001, said: "I didn't want to carry around the stigma of a life-long disease that would define me and potentially end my career. ... I was so terrified of losing everything, I convinced myself the only way to deal with this, was to not deal with this.

Until recently, I lived in denial and isolation, and in constant fear, someone would expose me. It was too heavy a burden to carry, and I simply couldn't do that anymore..."

This would explain Mariah's complete and total denial that she ever had a relationship at all with Eminem. If she could brand him a sleazy liar, who never touched her, then anything else he said about her behavior would also come into question. She doubled down and told Oprah that their friendship was only ever platonic, and that she could count the men she slept with on one hand and that Eminem wasn't even on that hand.

She told the press she was like Mary Poppins in relationships very prim regarding sex.

Mariah's fear of Eminem outing her unstable behavior, seemingly led to her dissing him and denying they were more than platonic friends in several interviews.

Eminem hit back at the interviews on his 2002 song Superman about the women he met in strip clubs who tried to become more *"What you trying be? My new wife? / What, you Mariah? Fly through twice."* And in the song *When the Music Stops* also on his album *The Eminem Show*.

> *I done came way too far in this game to turn and walk away and not say what I got to say. What the fuck you take me for a joke? You smokin crack? Before I do that, I'd beg Mariah to take me back.*

Mariah denied their relationship again on Larry King Live:

> "I hung out with him; I spoke to him on the phone. I think I was probably with him a total of four times. And I don't consider that dating somebody."

The Eminem Show was released in May of 2002. In December 2002, Mariah's album *Charmbracelet* came out on which she hit back fiercely. Unlike Eminem, who had only mentioned her briefly in a couple of songs, she wrote a whole song for Marshall that was savage called *Clown*.

> *I should've left it at, how ya doing?*
> *I should've left it at I like your music too, and*
> *I should've never called you back when you pursued me*
> *I should've never given you my fucking two way*

The insults don't end there.

> *You should've never intimated we were lovers*

> *When you know very well, we never even touched each other*

> And

> *I gotta break it to ya delicately, dummy*
> *Taking my G5 twenty minutes wasn't nothing*
> *But I guess you wouldn't know that's the way I roll*
> *Consequently, now your ego's fully overblown*
> *You don't want the world to know that you're just a puppet show*
> *And the little boy inside often sits at home alone*
> *And cries, cries, cries, cries*
> *Who's gonna love you when it all falls down, and*
> *Who's gonna love you when your bankroll runs out?*
> *Who's gonna care when the novelty's over?*
> *When the star of the show isn't you anymore*
> *Your pain is so deep-rooted (Nobody)*
> *What will your life become?*
> *Sure, you hide it but you're lost and lonesome*
> *Still just a frail shook one*

Mariah's G5 was the helicopter she took from New York to visit Marshall in Michigan.

In 2003 Mariah parodied Eminem on tour. Putting on a marionette show in which she showcased Eminem puppets.

Eminem responded to Mariah's Marionette Show diss on his own *Anger Management Tour* by playing voicemails alleged to be from Carey.

> "I heard you were getting back with your ex-wife. Why won't you see me? Why won't you call me?"

A "friend" of Carey's claimed to the press they weren't really her.

In 2009 Mariah married Nick Cannon around the time Eminem's first studio album in five years came out and he made fun of the pair, and Mariah's alleged alcoholism on his song *Bagpipes from Baghdad*

Locked in Mariah's wine cellar all I had for lunch
Was red wine, more red wine, and Captain Crunch
Red wine for breakfast and for brunch

The references to Mariah in *Bagpipes from Baghdad* led to Mariah's song and video *Obsessed*.

As brutal as Mariah's lyrics had been on *Clown*, there was no music video. Because *Obsessed* had a music video with Mariah dressed up like Eminem, in a hoodie and sweats, this second song got way more attention. This was Mariah's second full song about Eminem. A response to the silliness of *Bagpipes from Baghdad*.

"Why are you so obsessed with me? Boy, I want to know. Lying that you're sexing me
When everybody knows, it's clear that you're upset with me
Ohh, finally found a girl that you couldn't impress
Last man on the earth, still couldn't get this?"
(Mariah Carey - "Obsessed")

It was this song that led to Eminem's first full song about Mariah *The Warning*. A diss track in which he calls her both psycho and an alcoholic.

Like I've been going off on you all this time for no reason.
Girl you out ya alcoholic mind. Check ya wine cellar.
Look at the amounts of all the wine.
Like I fucken, sit around and think about you all the time.
I just think this shit is funny when I pounce you on a rhyme.

A babysitter of Hailie's claims that in 2001, she heard Eminem tell Mariah on the phone repeatedly that he loved her and that he would complain that Mariah would frequently say to him, "I love you, but you don't love me."

However, while Mariah may be lying that there was no romance, even Eminem's own songs indicate that she may not be lying that there was technically no intercourse.

In his 2009 song *The Warning* he directs lines to her new husband, Nick Cannon,

Made me put up with her psycho-ass over six
months and only spread her legs to let me hit once
Yeah, what you gonna say?
I'm lucky?
Tell the public that I was so ugly that
you fucking had to be drunk to fuck me?
Second base? What the fuck you tell Nick, pumpkin?
In the second week, we was dry humping,
It's gotta count for something
Listen girly, surely you don't want me to talk about
*   how I nutted early 'cause I ejaculated prematurely*
and bust all over your belly,
and you almost started hurling and said I was gross,
*   go get a towel, your stomachs curling.*

Or maybe you do.
But if I'm embarrassing me,
I'm embarrassing you and don't you dare say it isn't true.

By Eminem's own admission, it seems their sexual relationship didn't go very far. While Nick Cannon wrote on his personal blog that Mariah had told him Eminem never go to second base with her. Eminem claims they made out heavily and attempted to have actual intercourse seemingly only one time.

Later in this song, Eminem says

How many times you fly to my house? Still trying to count
Better shut your lying mouth if you don't want Nick finding out
You probably think 'cause it's been so long
if I had something on you, I woulda did it by now
Oh, On the contrary, Mary Poppins
I'm mixing our studio session down and
sending it to mastering to make it loud
Enough dirt on you to murder you
This is what the fuck I do!
Mariah, it ever occur to you that I still have pictures?

Tellingly this was pretty much the end of the beef. Mariah never responded.

The fact that Mariah finally reached acceptance of her condition and started medication in 2017 might explain why in 2017 sources revealed to Life and Style magazine that Mariah Carey's people were suddenly trying to get in touch with Eminem's people about burying the hatchet.

Unfortunately, Eminem's people were suspicious and told Mariah that she'd have to ring him herself. Staff told Life and Style, "we smell a publicity stunt."

Life and Style labeled this a diva moment, imagining that Carey refused to stoop to making phone calls herself out of vanity.

But Mariah was trying to contact Marshall sixteen years after he changed all his phone numbers to avoid her frightening phone calls. She may only have been being polite by reaching out to him, through his people, rather than frightening him by personally tracking him down. She may have wanted to apologize to him.

But back in 2002, after all the misery with Mariah, Eminem was about to try once more with another celebrity relationship.

<u>Eminem and Brittany Murphy</u> - Status Real Relationship

In November 2002, the movie *8 Mile* was released. Eminem told Asia MTV that he'd only wanted to dabble in movies and had had no idea about the serious amount of work and time he would need to put in to play the character of Jimmy "B-Rabbit" Smith Jr.

Kim Mathers made it clear to *Mojo in the Morning* that she wasn't thrilled with Brittany playing the role of Jimmy "B-Rabbit's girlfriend, and it was clear that Kim considered herself prettier than Brittany. Mojo on *Mojo in the Morning* described it as Brittany playing Kim even though the plot of the movie was meant to be fictional. *8 Mile* mirrored Marshall's life in so many ways a lot of people didn't seem to accept that it was still a fictionalized tale.

Everyone loved Brittany on the set of *8 Mile*. Reportedly

she was bubbly and fun. Brittany left love notes on Eminem's mirror with little lipstick kisses.

Brittany would play with Hailie jumping around and singing with hairbrushes. Hailie had seen *Clueless* and was thrilled to play with the star.

One day, Eminem returned to his trailer on the set of *8 Mile* and found Hailie and Brittany asleep in his bed. Exhausted himself, he climbed in. This led to a furious Kim when Hailie reported the scene back to her Mom.

Sadly, Eminem's complaint to *Mojo in the Morning,* regarding how celebrities he'd dated were all crazy, unfortunately, echoed in his relationship with Britney.

Eminem held a big party for the cast of 8 Mile complete with a bunch of women from the local strip club, Brittany allegedly got jealous, and she was annoyed by all the strippers hanging around Marshall. It has been alleged that Brittany faked a seizure.

Once she had him alone, Brittany started talking to him normally, and she and her mother refused to let Marshall call 911.

This second incident of celebrity craziness made Marshall break off the relationship and made the young man even more cynical. He reportedly stopped dating altogether and admitted to admitting to the press that he only visited strip clubs to satisfy his needs.

That was until 2005 when he fell in love with Kim all over again.

EMINEM AND KIM- STATUS Ex-Wife and Co-parent. Possibly still together.

One thing to remember about Kim Mathers is that she has

overcome both cocaine and alcohol addiction. To *Mojo in the Morning,* Kim credited her recovery to the prison sentence she served that lasted from February 2004 to October 2004. Mojo himself backed Kim up on the radio, telling the world he had partied with Kim since her release, and she was clean.

Kim, with her beauty and fame, might have had a career as a celebrity, but instead, she has devoted herself to raising five children.

Although some articles and blogs claim that Kim is an illustrator of greetings cards, children's books and puzzles. A simple look at the website shows that http://kimberleyscottillustrates.blogspot.com/ is owned by a woman who lives in London and happens to also be called Kimberly Scott. This is clearly not Hailie's mother as she lives in Michigan never far from Eminem so that the two can co-parent.

The other Kimberly Scott has several children's books published by the traditional publisher *Raintree,* but Eminem's Kim may have published one children's book under the name Kimberly Ann Scott with the notorious vanity publisher AuthorHouse.

While this book *Mommy! There's a Snot Man Standing Next to You!* Published in 2009, the book is a story to teach children to use tissues or a handkerchief.

Unfortunately, using a vanity publisher that is known for having numerous lawsuits against them and innumerable complaints on online sites such as *Pissed Consumer* may have put Kim off writing further books, or the author may be yet another Kimberly Ann Scott and not Eminem's Kim at all.

Eminem and Kim first met in 1988. Marshall was fifteen. Eminem told *Rolling Stone*

> "I met her the day she got out of the youth home. I was at a friend's house, and his sister was friends with her, but she hadn't seen Kim in a while 'cause she was in the youth home. And I'm standing on the table with my shirt off, on top of their coffee table with a Kangol on, mocking the words to LL Cool J's "I'm Bad." And I turn around, and she's at the door. Her friend hands her a cigarette. She's thirteen, she's taller than me, and she didn't look that young. She easily coulda been mistaken for sixteen, seventeen. I said to my friend's sister, "Yo, who was that? She's kinda hot." And the saga began. Now there's the constant struggle of "will I ever meet somebody else that's gonna be real with me, as real as I can say she's been with me?"

Kim Scott and her twin sister Dawn were born on Jan. 9, 1975, to Kathleen Sluck in Warren, Michigan.

At age twelve, the twins decided to run away from an allegedly alcoholic and sexually abusive stepfather and settled for a while at a youth shelter outside of Detroit.

Eminem's mother, Debbie Nelson Mathers, who at twelve had allegedly also been almost sexually assaulted by her own stepfather and had seen her stepfather dragged away in handcuffs by police, took an interest in the young girl.

Debbie claims that Kim told her she had been raped by her stepfather and forced to sleep with other relatives. Debbie took the runaway girl in.

Eminem's mom explains in her book that she was excited at first to have a "daughter" and keen to foster Kim and look after her. Kim lied to Debbie, telling her she was fifteen like

Marshall, and Debbie believed her until the truant officer turned up and told Debbie that Kim was only thirteen.

Debbie says she attempted to keep Kim sleeping on the couch in a room outside her door and Marshall in an upstairs bedroom in the Dresden Street home she had bought. But Debbie claims Kim later bragged that she'd slipped upstairs to seduce Marshall.

Some victims of child sexual abuse develop hypersexuality and sex addiction as a result of their experiences. This plus cocaine and alcohol addiction may be at the root of some of the accusations of promiscuity leveled against Kim Mathers.

It is, of course, not known if Kim was teasing Debbie about having seduced Marshall when she was a young teen, it's possible Kim was only taunting Debbie, or that Debbie made the whole thing up or that Debbie misremembers what her daughter-in-law said. Or it might be true. Regardless it seems clear that both Marshall and Debbie believed at first that the nearly six-foot Kim was fifteen.

Debbie even claims she had baked a cake and celebrated Kim's "sweet sixteen" three or four days before the truancy officer turned up and told her Kim was thirteen.

Once Debbie learned that Kim was only thirteen, she tried to break the couple up. When this proved ineffective, she hoped that their puppy love would die out. To her surprise, it never did.

Marshall dropped out of school in 1989. He began working with his friend Mark Ruby as a dishwasher and short-order cook at Gilbert's Lodge and recording songs in Mark Ruby's basement. It was here the notorious song *Ole Foolish Pride* was recorded.

It is believed by some that the black girlfriend he sings

about in *Ole Foolish Pride* may be the same girl he admits to cheating on Kim within the song *Kim*.

He sings about this other girl again in his 2004 song *Yellow Brick Road* from his *Encore* album.

> *And there was this black girl at our school, who thought I was cool*
> *'Cause I rapped, so she was kinda eyein' me*
> *And oh, the irony, guess what her name was?*
> *Ain't even gonna say it, plus*
> *The same color hair as hers was and blue contacts*
> *And a pair of jugs, the bombest goddamn*
> *Girl in our whole school, if I could pull her, not only would*
> *I become*
> *More popular, but I would be able to piss Kim off*
> *At the same time, but it backfired*
> *I was supposed to dump her, but she dumped me for this black guy*
> *And that's the last I ever seen or heard*
> *Or spoke to the "Ole Foolish Pride" girl,*

While working at *Gilbert's Lodge,* Marshall would go to *The Hip Hop Shop* on Saturdays to perform in rap battles.

The Hip Hop Shop in Detroit was a clothing store owned by fashion designer Maurice Malone who hosted open mic nights. The open mic nights and rap battles were managed and hosted by Proof on Saturdays from 4:00 - 6:00 P.M. The Hip Hop shop closed down in 1997 because Malone and his partner Jerome Mongo decided to move to New York and focus on the clothing line.

So, from 1989 to 1999, Marshall's life consisted of loving his girl Kim. Breaking up and getting back together with her on and off and performing at the *HipHop Shop* on Saturday nights but spending his days washing dishes and flipping burgers as a short-order cook.

Kim's enemies, such as Marshall's mom and Hailie's former babysitter, love to claim Kim would taunt Marshall about his dreams of becoming a local rap star, by telling him during drunken rages. that he was a nothing and a nobody, just a burger flipper.

During the years 1988 to 1999, Kim and Marshall would frequently break up but then get back together.

In the 2000 song, *Kim* Marshall admits to cheating on Kim at the age of eighteen.

> *You really fucked me, Kim!*
> *You really did a number on me!*
> *Never knew me cheatin' on you would come back to haunt me*
> *But we was kids then, Kim, I was only eighteen*
> *That was years ago, I thought we wiped the slate clean*
> *That's fucked up! (I love you!) Oh God, my brain is racin'*
> *(I love you!) What are you doing? Change the station!*

The cheating he mentions may have been with the black girl, also named Kim, who is mentioned in the song *Yellow Brick Road*. The songs *Just the Two of Us* later name changed to *97 Bonnie and Clyde* and the song *Kim* all imply that Kim got revenge for the cheating Marshall did in 1989 by cheating on him with someone in 1996.

Songs are not always autobiographical, but in Eminem's case, they very often are. In these three songs, Eminem sings about killing Kim, her "husband," and her four-year-old stepson. It appears Kim may have had a relationship with a man with a four-year-old in 1996 though there is no evidence that she has ever married anyone but Marshall. Possibly she was engaged to this man.

In any event, it seems Marshall fantasied about how furious he'd be if Kim actually married this other man.

Kim admitted to *Mojo in the Morning* that the couple had got back together over and over despite infidelities on both sides.

Kim was frustrated by their living conditions during the years 1990 to 1997. Sometimes the couple lived with Marshall's mom, but according to Kim on local Detroit radio show *Mojo in the Morning*, Debbie would stalk around the house shaking it, throw hairbrushes at them, and have rapid mood swings from being sweet and kind to yelling torrents of abuse and kicking them out.

Kim also told *Mojo in the Morning* that Debbie would constantly accuse her, Marshall, and Nathan of stealing things. An accusation backed up by Marshall, Nathan, and Hailie's former babysitter Jenny Watkins.

Sometimes Marshall and Kim would go back to stay at Kim's mother's house, but Kim's parents thought Marshall was low life trash and would fight with Kim about it until one day Kim's stepfather chased Marshall out of the house with a gun and told him to never come back.

Eminem mentions this on his 2000 song *Marshall Mathers*

> *Now everybody's so happy and proud*
> *I'm finally allowed to step foot in my girlfriend's house (Hey!)*

In 1993 little Alaina Scott and her twin brother Adam

were born to Kim's twin sister Dawn. Adam was physically and mentally disabled; his father was given custody of him.

Kim and Dawn's mother, Kathleen Sluck, took on the responsibility of raising Alaina (then called Amanda) and was initially awarded custody of her. But according to Hailie's baby sitter Jenny Watkins she was allegedly verbally abusive to her granddaughter and playing bingo four or five nights a week, so Kim frequently cared for the child.

Eminem fell in love with the cute little girl and felt bad for her as he witnessed her grandmother being kicked from rental home to rental home and allegedly calling the little girl names when she was drunk.

Marshall told *Rolling Stone*: "I had a job and a car, and me and Kim, we bounced around from house to house, tryin' to pay rent and make ends meet. And then Kim's niece was born, which is my niece now through marriage. Watched her (Alaina) bounce around from house to house — just watchin' the cycle house to house — just watchin' the cycle of dysfunction, it was like, "Man if I get in position, I'm gonna stop all this shit. And I got in position and did."

Kim told *Rolling Stone,* "The neighborhoods we lived in fucking sucked. I went through four TVs and five VCRs in two years." Both Kim and Marshall told of the burglary where the thief at first only came in and made himself a sandwich.

"He left the peanut butter, jelly, all the shit out and didn't steal nothing," Eminem recalled. "But then he came back again and took everything but the couches and beds. The pillows, clothes, silverware — everything."

The music video for the 2004 song *Mocking Bird* shows home videos from those days with baby Hailie and toddler Alaina. The lyrics discuss the hard times Kim and Marshall suffered prior to 1999.

See Daddy had a job
But his job was to keep the food on the table for you and Mom
And at the time, every house that we lived in
Either kept gettin' broken into and robbed or shot up on the block
And your mom was savin' money for you in a jar
Tryin' to start a piggy bank for you so you could go to college
Almost had a thousand dollars, 'til someone broke in and stole it
And I know it hurt so bad it broke your momma's heart

Kim became pregnant unexpectedly at age twenty-one. Little Hailie was born on Christmas day 1995. After their baby was born, Kim and Marshall tried a lot harder to stay together for her sake at first. Trying to survive in Detroit on the wages of a short-order cook was hard for the couple with a little baby and often looking after a toddler as well.

Mike Mazur Eminem's manager at *Gilbert's Lodge* even recalls a six-month period shortly after Hailie's birth when Eminem gave up his music and worked 60 hours a week for six months. "He didn't want his daughter to grow up like he did, living from day to day and moving from week to week," Mazur says.

But giving up his music didn't last long. After six months of sixty-hour shifts as a short-order cook, Eminem was back at the HipHop Shop on Saturday nights.

The story of how Hailie's birth kicked Marshall into overdrive trying to make it as a rapper is well known. Marshall's ambition probably didn't extend further than becoming a big name in the rap scene in Detroit or maybe nationally. His first album Infinite came out in 1996.

A song on his album *It's OK* outlines his ambitions at the time.

> *One day I plan to be a family man happily married*
> *I wanna grow to be so old that I have to be carried*
> *Till I'm glad to be buried*
> *And leave this crazy world*
> *And have at least a half a million for my baby girl*
> *It may be early to be planning this stuff*
> *Cause I'm still struggling hard to be the man, and it's tough*
> *Cause man, it's been rough, but still, I manage enough*
> *I've been taken advantage of, damaged and scuffed*
> *My hands have been cuffed*
> *But I don't panic and huff, frantic and puff*
> *Or plan to give up, the minute shit hits the fan it erupt*

The hook for this song has lyrics that emphasize his daily grind raising money for his family.

> *It's a broke day, but everything is ok (It's ok)*
> *I'm up all night, but everything is alright (It's alright)*
> *It's a rough week, and I don't get enough sleep (I can't sleep)*
> *It's a long year pretending I belong here (Belong here)*

In 1997 Marshall released the *Slim Shady EP* his demo that eventually made it to Dr. Dre. This song contained the early version of his first song about killing Kim.

Lynn Hunt, who worked with Eminem at Gilbert's Lodge, told the *L.A. Times,* "I told him it was morbid killing your baby's mother. He told me, 'Yeah, but it will get me somewhere someday.'"

The first song about killing Kim was initially titled *"Just the Two of Us."* There is no doubt the song among others did impress Dr. Dre. The original title made the song a parody of a song by Will Smith that was also called "Just the Two of Us.". (Will Smith song being a happy song that was only about his love for his son.)

DJ Jazzy Jeff made friends with Eminem in Detroit, back before Eminem became famous, and invited Marshall for a visit to Philadelphia in 1997. Jazzy told *Hip Hop DX,* "we went in the studio, and just knocked out some stuff. It was crazy because that was one of the (rare) times that Will (Smith) was in town. Will walked into the room, and I think I played Will '*Just the Two of Us.*'" The song with the same name as Will's own song.

"Will listened to it, and Will looked at him and said, 'You're either gonna be the biggest flop in Hip Hop, or you're gonna be the biggest thing that we've ever seen in Hip Hop.'"

Referring to Marshall's song about being alone with his toddler daughter after kidnapping and murdering his wife, Jazzy Jeff said, "It was so outrageous 'You're gonna be the biggest flop' because I guess people are just gonna think you're so crazy. Or you're just a super genius'—and the super genius part really paid off."

The Slim Shady EP of 1997 that contained "Just the Two of US," was the demo tape that inspired Dr. Dre to invite Marshall back to his studio.

The Slim Shady LP (that contained the song 97 Bonnie and Clyde) sold 480,000 copies in its first two weeks.

Baby Hailie's vocals even feature on the track, with Eminem later recalling in interviews "I lied to Kim and told her I was taking Hailie to *Chuck E. Cheese* that day. But I took her to the studio. When she found out I used our daughter to write a song about killing her, she fucking blew. We had just got back together for a couple of weeks. Then I played her the song, and she bugged the fuck out."

Former co-workers at *Gilbert's Lodge*, where Marshall worked as a short-order cook, remember Eminem agonizing in 1997 over his battles with Scott. "He would come into work and worry and say, 'The bitch took my daughter and won't let me see her. I don't know what I'm going to do, I don't know what I'm going to do,'" restaurant manager Mike Mazur told *Salon* Magazine.

Even though Eminem wrote and published a song about killing Kim for his 1997 EP and his 1999 album, Kim and Marshall got back together in 1999 and married that year. Their wedding date was June 14th, 1999.

Kim explained to *Mojo in the Morning* that she wanted to get married in 1999 in the hopes that it would keep Marshall faithful to her while he was on tour, but that that didn't work out. Eminem's security guard confirms Marshall's unfaithfulness in some detail in his book.

In fact, during Eminem's first tour, he was not just sexually unfaithful to Kim with groupies, but also emotionally unfaithful with a woman he met named Kesia Alvarez with whom he had a full-blown affair. Never-the-less, Kim and Marshall remained married until 2001 with Eminem's staff frequently hiding girls from Kim and flying them home whenever she decided to show up. Phone calls from Kim would often lead to Marshall turning groupies away that he had been about to have sex with.

One time Kim found a message on Eminem's phone from Kesia, and she understandably flipped out, so the whole crew made up a lie that Kesia was a stalker. The entire crew was reportedly fond of Kesia and wanted to protect her from Kim, so they told her it was a stalker named Amy that called every hotel. Kim didn't really buy it but accepted it.

Eminem told a Detroit newspaper in 2000 that he "always wished for (success), but it's almost turning into more of a nightmare than a dream." He noted that his marriage was suffering as a result of his career.

Marshall seemed torn between wanting to provide a happy traditional home life and marriage for Hailie and wanting to enjoy the perks of being a superstar. Adding to his troubles was Kim's alcoholism and the beginning of his own, causing drunken fights between the two. However, the married couple bought a house together that year.

Eminem told *Spin* magazine about how inappropriate the first house he and Kim bought in the heart of Detroit turned out to be. At the time, he just realized he had a lot of money, and it made sense to build a house, but he didn't truly understand his level of fame.

The first house was on a main road across from a trailer park. People would leave M and M rappers on the lawn and scream out to them from their cars all day and night. Kids from the trailer park would sneak in their back yard and jump in their swimming pool. The "No Trespassing" signs were stolen. The mailbox was sawed off and stolen. Eminem told the press that he hadn't realized the trailer park was in the back of the house and had not chosen such a house on purpose.

In the book by Byron Williams, *Shady Bizzness: Life as*

Eminem's Bodyguard in an Industry of Paper Gangsters, Eminem's former bodyguard" claims that Kim in the year 2000 was "more hardcore and gangster than 95 percent of rappers in the industry".

According to both Big Naz and also Hailie's babysitter, Kim once ripped off her sister's dress during a drunken fight and then threw her naked twin sister out of a slow-moving limo. Talking about this incident to *Mojo in the Morning,* Kim claimed she did also throw out some of her mother's clothes that were in the car for Dawn to wear.

Dawn initially laid a police complaint but later dropped it. Kim claimed Dawn had been high and had started the fight by punching Kim in the face for no reason. Kim and the taxi driver left Dawn in Canada that day as they had been on a drive to visit bars over the border.

Eminem's bodyguard also claimed Kim in the year 2000 was prone to drunken violence.

"I saw her throw a lamp at Eminem on a tour bus, knocking him down." Another time Williams claimed Kim smashed Marshall's head into a mirror. Williams claimed, "Man, he is terrified of her. She is one tough lady and bigger than him."

Kim is at least five foot eleven if not six foot while Eminem is reportedly only five foot eight.

Eminem's uncle Todd Nelson was once interviewed in a documentary entitled *"The Real Slim Shady."* Todd claimed that Kim had a sexual hold on Marshall because of her bisexuality and that she would bring random women home from clubs to share with Marshall, which gave him a thrill.

Todd Nelson, Debbie's brother, claimed, "Why would you not want a wife that has other women waiting for you? It's every man's dream, right?"

However, Kim's former best friend and Hailie's babysitter Jenny Watkins claims that Marshall was actually upset to come home and find Kim fast asleep in bed with a naked woman. Watkins claims Kim would hang out sometimes at the Rainbow Room, a gay club in Detroit. Kim admits that in those days, she made many mistakes due to her addictions.

The baby sitter also claimed that Kim was very verbally abusive to Eminem at times during drunken rages, often telling him he looked "like a drowned rat" and calling him rat boy.

Eminem admits to ripping a prenup up in 1999. Something he was later to regret. He admits to this in his 2002 track *Hailie's Song,* a song he originally wrote just to share with Hailie when she got older.

The song was about how happy he was with the shared custody hours ordered by the court, how full of joy he was when Kim's appointed time with her was over, and he got her back for his hours. How glad he was that the court had awarded him shared custody with Kim since before this, it is alleged that Kim would hold Hailie like a weapon over his head, saying if he didn't clean up his act, he wouldn't get to see her.

An interview Kim had with *Mojo in the Morning* indicates that Patrick Scott was seven years old when Whitney was four. Patrick must have been born to Dawn around 1999.

At some point, the courts took Patrick away from Dawn because of her drug addiction lifestyle and gave joint custody of Patrick to Kim and Kim's mother, Kathleen Sluck.

When Kim was on the *Dr. Keith Ablow Show,* producers

played a 911 call in which Kathleen rang the police about Dawn kidnapping Patrick otherwise known as PJ.

In 2013 Kim had another child whom she named Parker. He is Hailie and Whitney's half-brother. A member of *D12* claims that Eminem adopted Parker in 2013, possibly wanting to keep all the half-siblings of his daughter with his daughter.

Was poor Kim unlucky in love again, or is this actually Marshall's child kept properly hidden from the public in a way Hailie never was?

In the year 2000, Eminem went on his first tour as a co-headliner. This was the *Up in Smoke Tour* (with Dr. Dre, Snoop Dogg, Ice Cube, and others.)

Kim was left alone, raising Hailie and Alaina. She later told the *Dr. Keith Ablow Show,* "When Marshall's first tour started is when his ego just went "poof," like he was God, that's what he thought... I was just told that I should be grateful that he still talks to me, you know how many women throw themselves at him. And I just pretty much felt like a piece of crap."

In the summer of 2000, Eminem did a couple of things that almost led to him losing custody of his children. Upset and frightened after a falling out with his near seven-foot body guard. Marshall decided to go without security and carry a weapon instead.

Eminem claimed he caught Kim kissing a six-foot-two inches tall bouncer named John Guerra outside the Hot Rock Sports Bar and Music Café.

Guerra went to the police claiming that Marshall had pistol-whipped him with an unloaded gun, which led to felony concealed-weapon and assault charges. Guerra said, "I truly believe he was going to kill me. He was in such a rage. I actually lived through a nightmare and survived a nightmare."

Eminem admits this is true in the song *Cleaning Out My Closet*.

What I did was stupid, no doubt it was dumb
But the smartest shit I did was take the bullets outta that gun
'Cause I'da killed him, shit I would've shot Kim and him both
It's my life, I'd like to welcome y'all to "The Eminem Show."

According to Marshall, he did not hit Guerra with the gun but instead pulled out the unloaded gun, waved it around, and then hit Guerra with his fist.

D12 members Kuniva and Swifty McVay, agree that this was a period when Marshall would rant about how good his right hook was whenever he got drunk, which they thought was hilarious while on tour.

Being arrested on felony charges was serious, though. Marshall feared he could lose custody of his children. Only the day before the fight with Guerra Eminem had also been arrested during an altercation with Insane Clown Posse's road manager Douglas Dail at a car-audio store. "

In the end, Eminem pled guilty to the concealed weapons charges, and his plea deal meant the assault charge was dropped. He received a sentence of two years' probation.

Kim denied that she cheated on her husband in a letter to the Detroit Free Press:

"I don't think anybody in their right mind would cheat on a millionaire husband -- especially with a nobody at a neighborhood bar. My husband came up to *Hot*

Rocks to check up on me. Why is still unknown to me, because if I were to cheat on him, it wouldn't be in a neighborhood bar where he knows I am. Had he asked any questions before he flew off the handle, he would have realized that everyone with me, they were only friends. The fact that he just jumped to conclusions has gotten him and myself in trouble.

I would also like to state, since my husband has had no problem trying to make me look like an unfaithful wife, that every time I find a picture of him with other women, or read in magazines that he's involved with "groupies," I don't go and show up where he is making a huge scene and getting our faces to put all over the TV and papers. I have always taken his word on things and stood by his side."

In July 2000, Kim was in the audience for one of Eminem's concerts. During the performance, he hit a blowup doll that resembled her. Kim went home after the show and attempted to take her life.

She recalled the incident for Dr. Keith Ablow in 2007:

"Seeing the crowd's response and everybody cheering, singing the words and laughing, and it just felt like everyone was staring at me. I knew that it was about me."

There have been many arguments among fans about what actually happened. There has often been an assumption that Eminem was performing the violent 2000 song *Kim* his second song about killing her and the prequel to *97 Bonnie and Clyde,* however, no footage of Eminem performing *Kim* while beating a blow-up doll appears to exist. Eminem had promised Kim that he would never perform the song, and it appears that he did not; however, the music from the beginning of Kim was played during the *Up in Smoke Tour* before he switched to imitating his mother throwing him out of the house and then performed *Kill You* instead.

It is generally believed by fans that the blow-up doll that Kim saw him beating on stage was actually a doll whose face was made up like the hip hop group *Insane Clown Posse,* whom Eminem had a beef with and that Eminem was beating the doll to represent disrespecting that hip hop group. A Juggalo is a fan of the group *Insane Clown Posse* or any other *Psychopathic Records* hip hop group. Juggalos have developed their own idioms, slang, and characteristics. They put makeup on this face in a certain way which had been put on the blow-up doll.

Regardless Kim spoke to 20/20 about her feelings about Marshall writing songs about killing her.

"Here's this man who is supposed to be the man who loves me and protects me from being hurt (a husband), and here he is completely and totally disrespecting me in the worst way possible in front of billions of people. And in front of our kids, my family, my friends, now it just makes me angry because of what everyone thinks of me."

Eminem has expressed regret in his songs about the things his children had to go through at this time.

All the things growin' up as Daddy that he had to see
Daddy don't want you to see, but you see just as much as he did
We did not plan it to be this way, your mother and me
But things have got so bad between us, I don't see us ever bein'
Together ever again

Kim told 20/20 that Marshall had promised not to perform *Kim* while she was attending the concert and would be in the front row. She said that Marshall responded with, "Would I do that to you?"

She then told 20/20 that he did and that he beat a blow-up doll while performing the song.

She said people in the audience were pointing at her and laughing and that she got up left; the concert immediately got in a car accident on the way home, and then when she got home, slit her wrists in an attempted suicide. Kim had to have over three hundred stitches to fix her wrists.

However, Kim has since admitted that she's not sure which song he was actually performing.

It seems that Eminem may have played the music for the start of the song *Kim* but then switched to rapping *Kill You* and beaten the ICP doll as a diss to the group *Insane Clown Posse*.

Unfortunately, it seems Kim may have misunderstood the whole situation. *Kill You* is also violent about women, but is not specifically about Kim and is, in fact, more aimed at rage against his mother Debbie than anyone else.

It also ends with the words, "I'm just playing ladies, you know I love you." Regardless because of the intro music to the song *Kim* playing at the beginning, and Eminem performing *Kill You*, Kim misunderstood and believed he had lied to her about not performing the song. Tragically it seems she also misinterpreted the ICP diss with the blow-up doll as being about killing her.

Some of the audience members may have also misunderstood and believed the doll was her as she claims they were pointing at the doll and then pointing and laughing at her.

To the Detroit first responders that came to Kim's rescue from her suicide attempt, Kim would only say, "There has to be a better place than this."

Kim claims that Marshall's response to her 2000 suicide attempt was to come to the hospital and say, "I hope you don't expect me to cancel my tour."

Kim requested a divorce and sued him for emotional distress. Kim's lawyer, like Debbie's lawyer, chose to sue for the figure of ten million dollars. Kim sought full and permanent custody of four-year-old Hailie because of the lyrics of the song "Kim" as well as Eminem's onstage antics with the inflatable doll.

Surprisingly the lawsuit was settled, and the couple still lived together until 2001 when they officially divorced for the first time.

Marshall and Kim were given joint custody of their 5-year-old daughter, Hailie. Eminem retained ownership of their $450,000 home, and Kim got $475,000 to purchase her own house plus a six-million-dollar settlement.

It seems Kim is not very good with money as in 2019, she had an estimated net worth of only two million left. It must be remembered, however, that Kim has devoted almost her entire adult life solely to raising children of which she has custody of five, two of those children being her deceased sister's daughter Alaina and son PJ otherwise known as Patrick. He is Kim and Eminem's nephew. (Dawn's other son Adam, Alaina's twin brother, is cared for by his father.

A source claims he has physical and mental disabilities as a result of Dawn's addictions.) Kim's other son Parker was born in 2013 and is a half-brother to Hailie and Alaina. Kim told Mojo in the morning that he has autism. He is an adorable little boy, and pictures of Alaina hugging him can be seen online, and also some pictures of Parker with Kim, Whitney, and Hailie.

In June 2001, Macomb County Sheriff Mark A. Hackel told *Rolling Stone* that a Harrison Township resident called the police after a jet ski apparently broke down in a canal near Lake St. Clair. Upon checking the area, deputies from the sheriff's marine division saw two females carrying life jackets as they were walking down nearby Jefferson Avenue. It appeared both of them had been drinking.

The deputies could not issue an alcohol test because they had not witnessed either of them driving the jet ski. "We had no real legal means of trying to give them a sobriety or breath test because we don't have the right to do that, technically," Hackel told *Rolling Stone*.

However, they checked the women's drivers' licenses and found that both had outstanding warrants. Kim had an outstanding warrant for disturbing the peace. The detectives put Kim in a police car to take her to jail. They then noticed that a "white powdery substance of suspected cocaine" was found in the back seat of the police car where Kim had been sitting. Kim was in big trouble.

July 4, 2002 issue of *Rolling Stone* Eminem told the publication: "Kim is pregnant. I have no idea who the father is. I just know she's due any day. So, Hailie is going to have a baby sister. It's going to be tough the day she asks me why her baby sister can't come over. I've tried to keep her sheltered from those issues."

Kim told *Mojo in the Morning* that Marshall had a tough

time dealing with the idea of her being pregnant to another man and didn't know if he could be with her again after that.

However, Marshall got over this.

In 2004 he told *Rolling Stone*

> "Kim has been in and out of jail and on house arrest, cut her tether off, had been on the run from the cops for quite a while. Tryin' to explain that to my niece and my daughter was one of the hardest things I ever had to go through. You can never let a child feel like it's her fault for what's goin' on. You just gotta let her know: "Mom has a problem, she's sick, and it's not because she doesn't love you. She loves you, but she's sick right now, and until she gets better, you've got Daddy. And I'm here."

Kim's probation and home detention for cocaine possession turned into jail time after she cut her tether off and when on the run, possibly caused by the cocaine and alcohol addictions she has admitted to having at that time in her life. Her lover Eric Hartter worked as a tattoo artist, but he was allegedly a drug dealer, and while Kim was pregnant, he went on the run. He had two prior drug convictions and was charged with possession of the drug fentanyl. Kim went on the run too after cutting her ankle bracelet off and eventually was caught and sent to prison.

Strangely it was around this time that Eminem fell in love with Kim again. Possibly he felt sympathy and a connection because both had been through arrests and rehab.

Eminem had previously been terrified that he himself

would go to jail. But ultimately, he only got probation for the charge of carrying a concealed weapon.

Marshall had been terrified of losing his children. But in the end, he had managed to avoid doing any jail time for his crimes. He was given probation instead largely because there had been no bullets in the gun.

With Kim in jail, Marshall took full custody of his niece and Hailie. He also adopted Kim's baby girl Whitney to save the little girl from being placed in the foster care system.

Waiting at home for Kim to call the family from jail seemed to make him miss her more than ever before. Once Kim was released from prison, Eminem suggested she come stay with him and the kids for a week. The week stretched into a year.

Eminem told a local radio station, "'Me and Kim, we been through our dramas and shit, but I've been bald-faced lying if I said I don't love her or I'm with her because of my daughter. I'm with her, 'cause I really wanna be with her. I love that girl, man. I really do."

In his 2017 song *Bad Husband*, Eminem raps about Kim:

You were the beat I loved with a writer's block
The line that's hot, that I forgot
We laughed a little, cried a lot
I'll never forget when you came home, and you held
    Hailie
Day before you went to jail and daily
How we'd wait for that mail lady
Or by the phone, for mom to call
And I watched you pull yourself up, and we
    decided on
Givin' it one more try despite it all
You're my lightning rod when my sky gets dark

I'm your shiny rocks in that tiny box
When we tied the knot when we broke the knot

In 2003 Eminem wrote the sentimental song *Mockingbird* about their past, which came out in 2004 and between 2003 to 2006, the couple appeared to fall back in love.

The 2004 album *Encore*, however, confuses fans; even more, the sensitive, loving song *Mockingbird* is paired with another hate song about Kim called *Puke,* showing that the relationship had continued its ups and downs. Like *Kim*, the song *Puke* lyrics contain a confusing mix of love and hate.

I knew I shouldn't go and get another tattoo
Of you on my arm, but what do I go and do?
I go and get another one, now I got two, ooh
Now I'm sittin' here with your name on my skin
I can't believe I went and did this stupid shit again
My next girlfriend, now her name's gotta be Kim, shiiiiit
If you only knew how much I hated you
For every motherfucking thing, you ever put us through
Then I wouldn't be standin' here cryin' over you, boohoooo

Confusing fans, even more, was the music video for *When I'm Gone* with lines like

That's when I wake up, alarm clock's ringin', there's birds singin'
It's spring and Hailie's outside swingin'
I walk right up to Kim and kiss her, tell her I miss her
Hailie just smiles and winks at her little sister

Hailie, Whitney, and Kim were initially going to be in the music video, but after Kim found drugs and a gun in Eminem's room and they got into a fight, Kim told him she and Hailie wouldn't be in the video after all.

Kim told *Mojo in the Morning* that Marshall pigeon-holed her and told her, "If you have any doubts about marrying me again. If you don't want to set a date and have a wedding, then you can just pack your things and leave."

On September 14th, the couple announced to the public that they would marry again. Kim and Marshall had met on the fourteenth of the month back in 1988, and so for both their weddings and this announcement, they always chose the fourteenth of the month.

The two remarried in a beautiful wedding ceremony on January 14th, 2006; the marriage lasted only forty-one days as Eminem left the marital home on February 25th, 2006, never to return, and the couple officially divorced in April just days before Eminem's best friend Proof was murdered.

Kim expressed confusion and frustration to *20/20*, *The Keith Ablow Show* and *Mojo in the Morning,* telling them that she and Eminem had been through infidelities on both sides, been through beating each other up and yet they had finally fallen out permanently, seemingly over an argument she had with Nathan over a birthday party.

According to Kim, Nathan was disrespectful to her, and when she tried to chastise him, Marshall just walked out and never came back. Possibly watching Kim arguing with and scolding his little brother gave Eminem uncomfortable flashbacks to his relationship with his mom.

The death of his best friend Proof came quickly on the heels of the divorce, leaving a lot of pain. Even on the 2010 album *Recovery,* Marshall backs up Kim's 2006 complaints about his own behavior on the song *Going Through Changes*.

I lock myself in the bedroom, bathroom, nappin'
  at noon
Yeah, Dad's in a bad mood, he's always snappin'
  at you
Marshall, what happened that you can't stop with
  these pills?
And you've fallen off with your skills and your own
  fans are
laughin' at you
Know you just had your heart ripped out and crushed
They say Proof just flipped out, homie just whipped
  out and bust

Kim told the two TV shows and the radio show that she was finally speaking out because she no longer saw any hope for the two to ever date again. The two continued to maintain contact as co-parents, but during his worst period on drugs 2004-2007, Marshall reportedly wasn't doing a lot for his ex-wife and kids other than giving them tons of money.

Asked by Mojo of *Mojo in the Morning,* if Marshall was even clean during his early rehab attempts in 2006, Kim said: "I don't think so honestly."

This all finally changed after Marshall landed in the hospital in 2007, only two days away from death.

Eminem discussed his addiction to prescription medicine in a clip from the documentary *How to Make Money Selling Drugs,*

"I don't know at what point exactly; it started to be a problem. I just remember liking it more and more."

He revealed in this documentary that at the peak of his addiction, he was taking up to sixty Valium and up to thirty Vicodin pills a day.

After he nearly died and then got clean, Eminem was able to pull himself together and be a better father, co-parent, and rapper once again, putting out *Relapse* in 2009 and *Recovery* in 2010.

Eminem described how difficult it was for him to date during an interview with Rolling Stone in 2010.

> "As far as going out, like dinner and a movie — I just can't," he said. "Going out in public is just too crazy. I mean, I'd like to be in a relationship again someday. Who doesn't? It's just hard to meet new people in my position."

In 2013 Kathleen Sluck, Kim's mom, told the media Kim's mother, Kathy Sluck, recently revealed to RadarOnline.com that "The Monster" rapper and her daughter see each other "all the time" and "get along better than ever." He's currently building her a new mansion just five miles from his own house on Mile Road in Macomb, Mich.

Another source told how excited Marshall was about custom-building Kim, a beautiful mansion designed to his specifications for her.

> "She has been clean all these years, she just takes care of her family. She's doing very well," Kathy Sluck said. "I think they might get back together soon, they get on better than ever."

Sadly in 2015, Kim was arrested again on a DUI (driving under the influence).

Witnesses saw Kim drive her black Cadillac Escalade into a ditch, where it smashed into a pole and flipped upside down with her trapped inside.

In court, Kim said she was 'truly sorry' for her "selfish and destructive" actions. "" It was intentional," Kim told Detroit's Channel 995 radio show *Mojo in the Morning*.

"I never expected to make it out alive,' I have been clean for 10 years. I sat at the end of a road where I knew that no one else but myself would get hurt. I didn't take into consideration the safety of others and the feelings of my family, and I'm truly sorry."

She was sentenced to 12 months of probation and a $900 fine, which she immediately paid.

People complained about Kim's court documents being sealed and about her probation, accusing the courts of giving her special treatment. Kim went on Mojo in the Morning to deny this and explained that her court documents were sealed as they contained personal information about her health. As she had on 20/20 in 2006, she revealed once again that while it's lovely to have enough money to pay the bills and by her kids, whatever they wanted, that money wasn't everything and didn't make her happy. She told Mojo she was under stress caring for her youngest child who has autism and that she was in counseling for depression.

Here Eminem had a second chance to do right by his ex-wife, and he took it. Kim said he had been incredibly supportive, kind, and helpful.

Marie Hartter, Whitney's biological grandmother, told Radar Online that she thought Eminem and Kim had a shot at forever.

"They've been in love since they were fourteen or fifteen, and that's not going to stop any time soon. They will probably grow old together one way or another, as much as he says he hates her in his music; he loves her that much too, I feel. I think it's kind of like throwing gas on the fire.

I've always felt that that was each of their one true love. I think they met very young, they were together a lot of years, I don't think she's ever been with anyone for as long as she's been with him, whether it's off and on."

Is it possible that little Parker born in 2013, when Eminem had had so much time to reflect on the craziness caused in Hailie's life, by putting her in songs, might be Hailie's full brother? Rather than her half-brother? Is it possible that this boy whom a D12 member said Eminem immediately adopted is actually his son?

A tradesman who worked on the mansion Eminem had built for Kim also claimed in 2017 that Kim and Marshall were still together and in a secret relationship. This is, of course, just rumor and may or may not be false.

Perhaps Kim's suicide attempt in October 2015 would indicate that this story is not the truth. Kim has often stressed in the few interviews she has given that money isn't everything, and while it's fantastic that she never has to worry about bills and can get her kids whatever they want, that doesn't equal happiness.

Eminem and Kesia Alvarez -Status Real Relationship

During Eminem's early tours, he had a mistress called Kesia Alvarez, a manicurist from Florida, that the crew liked because they claimed she was more stable than Kim, and they didn't really regard her as a groupie.

Kesia met Eminem while he was signing autographs on Miami Beach in March 1999. She claimed later she was not a fan and only asked for his autograph for a laugh.

Alvarez has described the meeting this way. "As we faced each other, it was like, 'Wow!' We both felt it. We were staring at each other. He was very sweet and flirty. He has a very charming manner about him. Then he asked if I wanted to go to his show that night. "

Kesia refused to go on his tour bus with him, as she didn't want to seem like a groupie, but told him she'd drive down herself, and meet up with him. She didn't sleep with him for three days, then he started calling her and telling her he really liked her. 'I miss you. I really like you; I have to be in California next week, would you like to join me?" Kesia said, yes. She soon met Dr. Dre, and oddly, she claims Eminem introduced her to Dre as his wife.

Alvarez. claimed, "Marshall would call me her his Brazilian princess." Kesia's pet name for Marshall was 'My baby brat husband."

She claims he was a good kisser, but Kesia is very unflattering about everything else about their sex life. Although she claims to be in love with him and that he was with her. She claimed she had to teach him about sex. And as did Kim did at her most bitter, Kesia also claimed Marshall wasn't well endowed.

Eminem's bodyguard Big Naz Williams claimed in his book that Eminem started flying Kesia around in first-class to many different countries, while he was on tour causing outrage amongst his staff, because of the high price of first-class for Kesia, while his bodyguards etc....were refused raises being told the money wasn't there to spend on them.

Despite Kesia's assertion to the media that Eminem was in love with her, Eminem has stated in interviews that he's only ever been in love once-with Kim.

Eminem's former bodyguard and Kesia both accuse Eminem of allegedly sleeping with a 15-year-old girl called Agnes while on tour in Sweden, whom he initially thought was 19 because of her fake id. But Kesia and Nas allege that once the authorities contacted them regarding Agnes's mother being upset, Marshall didn't want to stop sleeping with her. Nas compared it to Eminem's rhymes regarding underage sex on the songs Guilty Conscience.

Eminem was overheard on the European tour telling Kesia that he was in love with her and that if it weren't for Hailie, he'd be marrying her (Kesia) instead of remarrying Kim.

However, it is alleged Eminem was on the club drug Ecstasy during that conversation. Later Marshall was drunk and high at the same time, and Kesia overheard him saying he didn't give a damn about either her or Agnes calling them both hoes.

After that, she wouldn't sleep with Eminem anymore, and he sent her home early from the tour after having spent seven grand on her tickets infuriating Proof who could not get a raise for all he did putting together the order of the all the shows and being the hype man.

Kesia got her revenge by telling the media that Eminem had premature ejaculation problems in his younger days (something Eminem admits himself in his song about Mariah Carey *The Warning*.)

EMINEM AND BEYONCÉ- STATUS Attracted but just professional

Asked if he'd ever dated Beyoncé, Eminem responded with, "I wish!" Their relationship was purely professional.

EMINEM AND RIHANNA Status Possible but Unconfirmed

A source who wished to remain private told contactmusic.com, "Marshall would date Rihanna in a heartbeat if she showed even the slightest interest. They're on the phone and texting each other constantly."

Eminem's grandmother Betty Kresin also tried to play matchmaker to the press telling *Heat Magazine* in 2010. "I can totally see what any girl, including Rihanna, would see in him. He's so charming; he has always had adorable, beautiful blue eyes and this charming, wonderful smile.

Rihanna would make a suitable partner for Marshall. But he needs to enjoy life and not get carried away with any relationships at the moment." But Rihanna was dating LA Dodgers baseball player, Matt Kemp, at the time. The press wanted to link Eminem and Rihanna romantically at that time because of their smash hit *Love the Way You Lie* that came out in 2010.

After that song was so successful in 2010. The pair were seen hanging out and hugging each other in 2012.

Eminem and Rihanna collaborated on *The Monster* in 2013, also a highly successful hit. And followed this up with a co-headlining concert tour called The Monster Tour in 2014, where they performed three songs together and many separately. The tour was a mini North American Tour, Eminem visited only California, New Jersey, and Michigan.

Eminem made some lewd comments about Rhianna in songs such as 2014s Shady XV that the media made much of, but there is no reason to assume the relationship was more than professional, and Rihanna is now dating billionaire Saudi businessman and philanthropist Hassan Jameel. Eminem's comment in the song *Killshot* that he left hickeys on Rihanna was almost certainly a joke response to Machine Gun Kelly's silly accusation on his song *Rap Devil* that Eminem would be too scared to ask Rhianna for her number. Ironically in the beef between Eminem and Machine Gun Kelly, the two men make sexual comments about women that neither man has ever slept with, i.e., Rhianna. Or in the case of Kim, a woman Eminem claims he hasn't slept within twelve years before the song's release.

<u>Eminem and Tara Reid</u> -Status Possible.

Marshall claimed to have slept with actress Tara Reid, star of the movies American Pie (1999), American Pie 2 (2001) and American Reunion (2012), and Bunny Lebowski in The Big Lebowski (1998).

He claimed to have slept with Reid in an interview on *Shade45*, where he also claimed to hit himself in the head with a hammer every night in order to get to sleep and other obviously ridiculous and untrue things.

However, he also listed Tara along with Mariah and Britney Murphy in the same sentence, and his relationships with Mariah and Britney are verifiable.

Tara Reid said she has dated "a million guys," so possibly Eminem was one of them, although there is no other solid evidence. It seems they may have had a one-night-stand.

<u>EMINEM AND MARNI Bright-</u> Status Professional Relationship, Romantic Relationship Unconfirmed

Marni Bright is vice president of artist relations for *Jeff Bass Music* in Detroit.

For a while, the paparazzi having seen Eminem and Marni walking around town together, posted short snippets claiming these two were an item.

However, both Marni, Eminem, and Eminem's publicist repeatedly said it was only a working relationship. The whole rumor appears to have started just because someone saw Eminem and Marni at the studio together in 2007 and tracked down who she was.

<u>EMINEM AND TRACY McNew-</u> Status Professional Relationship. Possible Romantic Relationship but denied by all.

Eminem mentions Tracy McNew in the song *It's Been Real*, which Celeb gossip mags jumped on and made much of, but there is nothing in what he said to indicate a romantic relationship. He merely thanks all the significant people that helped him including Dre, Jimmy Iovine, "the whole Shady staff," then includes

> *Paul Rosenberg, Tracy McNew*
> *You know I love you guys*
> *I couldn't do it all without you*

Tracy being the one female name, sent the tabloid and celeb mags into a desperate attempt to claim her as a girlfriend.

Marshall publicist and McNew herself denied the rumor.

However there has been plenty of speculation that Tracy was the "life coach," Kim's sister Dawn claimed he was having an affair with. Speculation has also fallen on Marnie Bright.

<u>Eminem and Gina Lynn-</u> Status- Completely False tabloid invented rumor and clickbait.

The rumor that Gina Lynn had briefly been Eminem's girlfriend was made up by the paparazzi after she appeared in his 2003 music video for his song *Superman*.

However, Lynn told the press that while she had gone back to Eminem's room after the video, that his six and even seven-foot-tall black bodyguards showed no sign of leaving his bedroom, making her feel intimidated. (Lynn mentioned their race.)

Lynn explained that she didn't want to get intimate in front of them. And in addition, Lynn said that while Marshall was nothing but sweet, polite and complimentary, Lynn still felt intimidated due to the vicious lyrics of the song *Superman* itself.

Lynn said she worried what he might say about her in a song later if she slept with him. So, while he showed interest in having sex with her, she demurred and left the room. So, though you will frequently see pictures of Gina Lynn and Eminem together that are taken directly from the Superman music video or publicity stills from around that Gina Lynn did not have so much as a one-night-stand with Eminem, although according to Lynn he did attempt to make that happen.

———

Eminem and Skylar Grey- Status- Unlikely.

Skylar Grey is responsible for writing the hook for one of Eminem's most popular hits, the 2010 song *Love the Way You Lie*. It is possible that Grey, in denying they'd ever been involved, was sticking to Eminem's rumored "say no names" policy, but equally likely that they have always maintained a professional relationship.

Asked in an interview if they'd ever been romantically involved Skylar's response was very emphatic "No no no no no! It's all about the music, man. It's just about the music!"

———

Eminem and Sarah Ashley Toups, otherwise known as Sarati- Status-Fake, purely for promotional purposes for the album *Revival*.

Sarah Ashley Toups is an actress and fitness model, who appeared in a viral video where she filmed herself, and Eminem inside of a hotel room to promote the song *River*.

———

EMINEM AND NICKI MINAJ- Status completely false. A joke for publicity purposes.

The rumor started in 2018. Minaj captioned a clip with a lyric from her new single: "#BIGBANK OUT NOW @bigsean Told 'em I met Slim Shady. Bagged an EM!!!"

One follower was quick to reply, asking: 'You dating Eminem???' Minaj replied, 'Yes,' prompting her answer to receive thousands of likes.

Later, Minaj told TMZ reporters that it was all just a bit of fun and that she was only joking about dating Marshall.

She said Eminem played along with the joke, during a performance in Boston calling out to the audience "Boston, how many of you want me to date, Nicki Minaj?" He received a lot of screaming and catcalling.

"Well, goddammit, me too," he said. "Nicki, if you get this message, just text me later, we'll talk about it."

Later Nicki had to tell reporters that it was still only a joke but claimed she loved that Eminem was "goofy and fun like myself." All just another publicity stunt.

EMINEM AND BRITNEY SPEARS- Status- Appears to probably be a false rumor.

In an interview in 2006 on his own radio station Shade 45 Marshall told Lord Sear and Rude Jude's on their All Out Show that he had sex with Britney Spears but pulled out, that he regularly enjoyed taking heroin, and that he hit himself in the head with a hammer every night to get to sleep. Also, he wanted to make a New Year's Resolution "to try not lying."

Not much in that interview could be taken seriously.

Eminem also once gave a radio interview where he talked about how five-year-old Hailee loved to listen to Britney and was a huge fan, and Eminem said he thought her songs were corny and that she couldn't even sing. He even talked about how it kind of bothered him that his five-year-old daughter was watching someone who dressed so proactively. It seems very unlikely that they were ever involved.

GERI HALLIWELL & Eminem -Status True. It appears they did have a fling.

An insider is quoted by Britain's Daily Star newspaper as saying: "Backstage, someone asked Eminem what he thought about *The Spice Girls* reuniting for *Live 8*. Marshall responded that it was cool, but that the event shouldn't be focused solely on that.

Eminem then said he was hoping to meet 'the red-headed one" when he flew to the UK to play shows in September. He claimed he would call her when he got to Britain."

The Sun then reported that Eminem and ex-Spice Girl, Geri Halliwell had been meeting up regularly for cozy lunches and dinners after meeting by the pool of the Sunset Marquis Hotel in Los Angeles, where both were staying.

A friend of Halliwell, formerly known as "Ginger Spice," said, "You wouldn't expect them to have much in common — certainly in terms of their lifestyles. But their relationship seems to work. Geri is having a great time. She and Eminem have been out together ...bowling and for meals. Who knows whether it will lead to romance?" One of Eminem's memorable lyrics from his first break out 1999 hit was, *"I can't figure out which Spice Girl I want to impregnate,* "people joked that he had made his decision. The relationship did not appear to continue once Eminem left the UK.

As much as the public wants Marshall to be in a relationship, the reality may well be that he's been too much of an addict in one way or another to be in relationships much of the latter part of his life. According to *BuzzAngle Music's* 2018 Year-End Report, Eminem outsold every artist across the globe – in 2018 with a huge 755,027 album sales bagged, far ahead of second-place finishers BTS

Eminem's tenth studio album *Kamikaze* was only the tenth bestselling album; however, the findings show that it was Marshal Mathers' extensive back catalog that catapulted him to the top. He outsold The Beatles, Queen, and Taylor Swift for the year.

It seems Eminem traded in addiction to Valium, Ambien, extra-strength Vicodin, and alcohol for work-addiction, and in fact, Marshall admits this on *Kamikaze*. In the 2018 Kamikaze song Fall, Eminem says

> *"I got a marathoner's pace*
> *Went from addict to a workaholic, word to Dr. Dre*
> *In that first marijuana tape—guess I got a chronic*
>   *case (yeah)*
> *And I ain't just blowin' smoke, 'less it's in your*
>   *momma's face.*

Addiction Now is an online news resource for topics related to drug addiction, addiction treatment, and recovery. According to *Addiction Now,* workaholism is driven by a desire to mitigate negative feelings through avoidance and motivation.

In 1971, psychologist Wayne Oates created the word workaholism, he created the word based on alcoholism because of the similar negative consequences of both conditions.

It is estimated that about 10 percent of American workers

are workaholics, and this has been clinically associated with multiple adverse events, such as domestic conflicts, insomnia, as well as physical and mental health concerns.

In studies of workaholism, distinctions must be made between people who worked 50 hours a week or more because they were intrinsically motivated by their connections with work-related activities, and actual workaholism that is driven by a desire to mitigate negative feelings through avoidance and motivation. Certainly, Eminem loves hip-hop, enjoys being obsessed with hip-hop, and is motivated by his connections to work-related activities, but how much is too much? Where is the line?

A study conducted by researchers from New Zealand showed that longer work hours were associated with higher rates of alcohol-related problems, as well as more frequent alcohol use and higher rates of alcohol abuse or addiction.

The participants who worked more than 50 hours a week were 2 to 3 times more likely to have an alcohol problem than the participants who were not employed while the study was conducted.

Despite *Kamikaze* only being the tenth most popular album of 2018, because of his backlist and output, Eminem was by far the best-selling artist of the year. We can only guess what that means in relation to his tendencies towards obsessiveness and addiction and how healthy or unhealthy that is.

One thing is for sure, though, Eminem's prolific work output is the most plausible explanation for why no one can find any concrete evidence of Eminem having recent romantic relationships. And sadly, Kim Scott's suicide attempt in October 2015, makes rumors of a continued secret romantic relationship with Marshall seem less likely too.

CHAPTER SEVEN

I want the money, the women, the fortune, and fame.
That means I'll end up burning in hell scorching in
flames.

Eminem and Friends and Rise to Fame
(*Enemies, with Secret Identities.*)

According to *BuzzAngle* Music's 2018 Year-End Report, Eminem, at age forty-six years old, was the year's highest-selling artist in the world.

He outsold every artist across the globe – with a huge 755,027 album sales bagged, far ahead of second-place finishers BTS, who sold 603,307 albums

Kamikaze was only the tenth bestselling album; however, the findings show that it was Marshal Mathers' extensive back catalog that catapulted him to the top. He outsold The Beatles, Queen, and Taylor Swift.

But how did the story all begin, and who were Eminem's best friends along the way?

Eminem's love of hip-hop began at the age of eleven when his uncle Ronnie put Ice-T's song *Reckless* on the family record player. Eminem has said, "I thought it was the most incredible shit I'd ever heard."

His uncle Ronnie taught him how to rap. But it was in 1988 when Marshall was fifteen that Eminem became serious about rap as a career. He began rapping on community radio and was eventually heard by the Bass Brothers, who offered him studio space.

In 1989 Eminem's friend Mike Ruby, his rapping partner from a high school talent show, recommended that he join him washing dishes at *Gilbert's Lodge*, a rustic, family-style restaurant to earn some cash. Both young men were determined to be rappers and did not plan on making a career of the $5.50-an-hour gig. Eminem was later promoted to a short-order cook.

In 1990 Ruby received some money from an insurance settlement. Marshall and Mike Ruby began recording tracks in Ruby's basement. The future superstar was then calling himself M&M, later modified to Eminem. Ruby's professional name was Manix, and Ruby set up a basement studio that he dubbed Bassmint Productions, DeShaun Holton, known as Proof and James Deel, known as Chaos Kid formed the group *Soul Intent*. Later Eminem and Proof would leave this group to create the famous *D12*.

Eminem and Ruby created the now infamous track *Ole Foolish Pride,* a song Marshall recorded under his first name M and M.

This is a silly track in which a teenage Marshall disses a black girl that he had been dating. A girl ironically named Kim, who dumped him for a black guy.

This song recorded when Marshall was in his teens is the only known song where Marshall uses the "N-word" something Eminem has apologized for profusely both to the media and in the 2004 song *Yellow Brick Road*.

Shady records alleged copyright infringement over the two tracks. It turned out that one of the producers from the Bassmint days had an old tape with a bunch of recordings on it. The tape got left in a friend's car; the friend agreed to let someone sell it to *The Source* for sixty thousand dollars in exchange for half the money. *Shady Records* sued.

Some people wondered if Mike Ruby leaked the songs on purpose frustrated about being left behind, but there is no proof of this.

Other people claim it was actually James Deel, who allegedly sold the tapes for a half share of sixty thousand dollars to Eminem's enemy at *The Source* magazine, Benzino. After (possibly) selling the song Chaos Kid came out to the media to defend Eminem telling the press that Marshall wasn't a racist.

This may have been one of Deel's schemes to get Eminem to notice him and remember him again. Somehow Deel got left behind and wasn't invited to join Proof and Eminem as they formed their new group *D12*.

However, Deel has vehemently denied he sold the tapes. And has said he only agreed to be interviewed by the press to defend Marshall.

Eminem's very first performance of rap in front of other people was according to his mother at a talent show at *Centerline High School* with Mike Ruby known as Manix, his twin brother Matt Ruby known as Buttafingaz; and James Deel (Chaos Kid.)

In fact, Eminem, then known as M and M, performed

every year with Chaos Kid at *Centerline High School* in their yearly talent quests.

Debbie tells how Marshall wore all white with a jacket thnat he painted himself with the letters M and M as well as pictures he'd drawn of M and M candy. She said it's was James' school that they performed at and that the rapping was "good, clean, family fun." .

Late in his life, Deel had grown so desperate with poverty and "the grind" that he resorted to trying to contact his former friend and superstar through two public letters. (Just as Eminem's own mother and father had done.) These letters were very long and very intense and can be found in their entirety online.

Some interesting parts of the letters include the following

"Speaking of talent shows in a gymnasium," have you forgotten the lyrics to *Soul Intent*?

What's your Intent?

I'm analyzing every cut you're in to judge your intent.

I wanna know where you stand, I mean, as far as who you

are

How would you act if you woke up, and tomorrow, you're a

star?"

(And here's) lines from the last verse:

The rapper that's real is the one that stuck to his roots

Because they got ahold of him so much, they stuck to his

boots

> *And the only way to tell if he's really real is wait until he's*
> *made a mil*
> *And then you ask him if he still, and if he's real, then still he*
> will.
>
> Need I say more? Perhaps you have forgotten you said that, so it's just an error on your part that you left me behind?
>
> Because shit, homeslice, it's been twelve to thirteen years since you made your first mil, and you *still* ain't come around. Does it relieve your guilty conscience to blame it on me, the reason I've never "made it" by insinuating I'm lazy and have no motivation in the *Airplanes Pt. II* lyrics?"

Because Eminem happened to mention the school talent show in the song *Airplanes Pt. II*, James appeared to take Eminem's verses in the song personally.

Deel goes on to say, "You're taking the typical approach the rich take with the "pull yourself up by your bootstraps" philosophy. I believe it was MLK Jr. when speaking on the building of the beloved community who said, 'It's tough to pull yourself up by your bootstraps if you are bootless…'

People forget that one of our most celebrated American Heroes, Dr. MLK Jr., was not… a supporter of the capitalist system. In fact, he was very critical in denouncing it. You'll notice how he makes reference to how black people were not given any land when they were "freed." But the truth of the matter is, that is the current state of the vast percentage of America's people regardless of color, and in this current economic crisis, which is the result of the never-ending greed of corporations, every 7 seconds someone loses their home in this country."

Sadly, on September 28th, 2011, Chaos Kid killed himself at age 37, no one found his body for six days.

Press articles on Deel's death included the following "In the late '80s, Detroit, Michigan's Chaos Kid served as one of the original members of Bassmint Productions, which included a young Eminem. The two later recorded under the name *Soul Intent* from 1989 to 1992.

Proof's funeral was one of the few funerals Eminem ever attended, usually citing that he did want to turn the funeral into a circus by his presence. (But also, probably having too much work on.) He sent flowers and a card to Deel's family instead.)

However, in 2017 Eminem possibly paid a small tribute to Chaos Kid in the song *Untouchable*

Single mother strugglin' through substance abuse
While people with nothin' to lose shoot each other for
shoes
Fuck your Republican views
Pull ourselves up by our bootstraps, where the fuck
are the boots?

Did Chaos Kid inspire this line? It's hard to say. The song is more about the bad treatment of African Americans by the police than it is about poverty in general.

Deel complained in his open letters that Eminem had lost interest in him completely when James lost interest in hip hop.

Eminem's grandmother told a similar story about Eminem losing interest in Ronnie when Ronnie lost interest in hip hop. And indeed, once Ronnie told Marshall that he was into heavy metal now and had given up on the idea of being a rapper, Marshall fell out of touch with him. Betty had complained Marshall hadn't seen Ronnie for years prior to his death.

This appears to be a pattern; a friend loses interest in hip hop, and Marshall loses interest in the friend. This might appear cold. But maybe not if you consider Marshall single-mindedness about using hip hop to make money for Nathan, Hailie, and Alaina in his younger days. Also, it seemed Marshall just preferred to hang out with people who shared his overwhelming passion.

Deel's open letter to Eminem was not a request for money, however, but a request to get in touch because Deel wanted to discuss with Marshall his "ideas" for helping people in Detroit. It seemed Deel mainly had dreams of Marshall getting him a job working to help reduce poverty in the city, which was his passion.

In his open letter he said:

"But it takes people like you - who actually have the expendable income to finance such endeavors to help get it started and to actually give a shit and sit down with a person like me and let's have some fun figuring out what's most important and what we can do. If you applied even just a fraction of your work ethic, passion, and talent you have for music towards social justice, just think of what we could do!

And that's what I don't get about you! You know I'm not just looking for a hand-out... But what's the purpose of me learning all this stuff if you're the one who's actually in a position of power to do something about it and you won't do *anything* about it? Do you realize how discouraging that is? To think of how much good you could do if your friend would only give a fuck about you and risk believing in you long enough to at least discuss it?

Do you even remember that for a couple of months I let Denaun (Mr. Porter now Eminem's hype man) live at our house in your room for free because I knew you guys were struggling to get *Infinite* recorded and I was doing my best to be a real soul bro? ... I don't understand you! So, what if our musical tastes diverged drastically, it isn't and wasn't about that. It's about being a good person."

Deel wrote his second angry open letter to Marshall in 2010, in which he suggested Marshall wasn't using any of his money for social justice. Deel suggested in this letter that Marshall open "*The Shady Foundation*" and let Deel help him with ideas for this charity.

It seems Deel was completely unaware that Eminem had actually started up the *Marshall Mathers Foundation* charity, as far back as 2002, into which Eminem pumped and still pumps a large chunk of his own personal income into the various works of that foundation.

With an estimated net worth of two hundred and ten million as of 2019, Eminem is the most successful white hip hop artist of all time. But Marshall seems to prefer to keep his charity work on the down low, either so as not to dent his bad-boy image, or just because he believes good works should be done in silence.

The *Marshall Mathers Foundation* funnels money into many different charities that help kids in crisis in Michigan. It supports college preparation programs and athletic programs for youth.

The foundation also provides funds for homeless shelters, AIDS charities, food banks, and all sorts of other good causes in the Detroit area where Eminem spent his teenage years.

Also, the *Marshall Mathers Foundation* provides money to the organizations *Families Against Narcotics*. And to *Common House*, which provides a lifeline for individuals and families in crisis, victims of crime, persons with mental illness, and people trying to cope with critical situations.

Eminem also supports arts organizations in Detroit, like the *Mosaic Youth Theatre of Detroit*. Also, Eminem has donated money to hurricane relief charities.

James Deel seems to have been aware of none of this. To be fair to Deel, it must have been a source of endless frustration that after six years of working off and on with Eminem (then M and M) and frequently sharing a house with him, Deel's interest in grunge and *Nirvana* was his undoing.

If only Deel hadn't become interested in other genres of music and stuck to hip-hop, he might have maintained his friendship with Eminem and had a place in his life, and as a result, a better income and a chance to fulfill his dreams of helping humanity.

Deel gave a timeline to *RapBasement.com* in which he explained that in 1993, he started to lose interest in hip hop becoming inspired by *Nirvana*, *Rage Against the Machine*, and *Arrested Development*.

Deel had a new desire to piece together a live band to help express his new musical vision. He still considered himself connected to *Bassmint Productions,* the makers of *Soul Intent*, but only loosely as he moved towards a more Grunge and Rock sound for himself. He remained friends with Eminem and continued to rent a house with him.

In 1995 Deel purchased a house on the East side of Detroit, and in 1996 Eminem moved in there as a rent-paying roommate.

After a while, Mr. Porter moved into Eminem's room, and Deel charged the two men no extra rent.

Like Eminem's mother, Debbie, who once owned the house on Dresden St, it seems Deel also eventually lost his Detroit home due to financial problems.

While Eminem's Denaun Porter on the other hand stuck with hip hop leading to the joys of *D12* not to mention becoming Eminem's hype man. Denaun is now estimated to have a net worth of two million today.

Meanwhile, Proof, who was a member of the original group *Soul Intent*, also had a job as Eminem's hype man and was believed to also have had a net worth of two million at his time of death. A far cry from the life of Deel, whose existence was one of continual financial struggles despite his undisputed writing and performing talents.

Like Deel, Eminem met Proof in high school. This lifelong friendship has been written about earlier in this book, including the man's tragic death at age thirty-two.

Denaun has also been named professionally as Kon Artis, and Denaun (often stylized as dEnAuN.)

Mr. Porter created all the beats on *Infinite*. But Proof came in at the last minute and said he didn't feel like the beats were banging enough. So, Proof brought in DJ Head's drum machine and put drums behind the song *Infinite* itself.

Eminem and Mr. Porter worked together as short-order cooks at a suburban Detroit restaurant called Gilbert's Lodge while starting *D12*. The two of them lived in an apartment on Runyon Ave. Marshall mentions the Runyon Ave Soldiers on *Like Toy Soldiers,* and *D12* have referred to themselves using the term on the songs *"40 oz"* and *"That's how."*

D12 is called *D12* short for dirty dozen. They were six members, each with a dual personality. The creation of each of their alternative personalities was the inspiration for Eminem's alter ego Slim Shady.

Eminem announced the end of *D12* as a group on the song Stepping Stones featured on his 2018 album *Kamikaze*. He laments that D12 as a group never felt right after Proof died and that it's not goodbye to their friendship but *D12* is over. He explains father in the song that he has found it too hard to shoulder expectations that he can help all of their solo careers.

Jeff and Marky Bass were two important early friends who discovered Eminem and believed in him when he was as young as fifteen. After hearing the teen rap on community radio, they offered him studio space and helped him put out *Infinite* and *The Slim Shady* EP. The Bass Brothers have been co-writers on many Eminem songs.

D12 was created by Proof in 1996. The original members of *D12* were Rufus Arthur Johnson is known as Bizarre, Denaun M. Porter, known as Mr. Porter, Von Carlisle known as Kuniva, and Karnail Pitts known as Bugz.

Eminem's friend Bugz was, unfortunately, another tragic story. In 1999 Bugz, who had just turned 21, yelled at a man who shot at his cousin with a water pistol.

A friend of the man with the water pistol responded by going to his car to get his real gun and shot Bugz and then ran him over. The ambulance took over thirty minutes before arrival, and Karnail died. Regarding his friend Bugz death, Proof was quoted as saying, "It just makes you look at life more serious." (sic)

After *Infinite* was mocked for being too positive and upbeat as well as too much like popular hip-hop artists AZ and Nas Eminem created a new character.

The original members of *D12* can be credited with giving Eminem part of the idea for Slim Shady. *D12* decided that the six of them would each take on an alter ego and call themselves The Dirty Dozen. The name *D12* later sprung from that. Eminem, having been mocked for being positive and upbeat, then got the idea to create a character that was based on every dark and evil thought that ever passed through his mind. Slim Shady was born.

Eminem's rhymes grew angrier after the album *Infinite* failed to sell, and he realized he needed an outlet. That's when Eminem created Slim Shady... while he was on the toilet.

To *Rolling Stone* he said

"Boom, the name hit me, and right away I thought of all these words to rhyme with it," he says. "So, I wiped my ass, got up off the pot, and, ah, went and called everybody I knew."

Slim allowed Marshall Mathers/Eminem to vent all of his angriest most vile thoughts in another persona. The other six members of D12 soon chose their own alter egos, so the group would have 12 members.

Around the time of Eminem's first record deal in 1999, Proof attempted to revive D12. He managed to recruit local Detroit hip hop duo *Da Brigade*, composed of Kuniva, a local MC, and Kon Artist.

More about Proof and Mr. Porter and the rest of D12 and their early years can be read about in Eminem's 2008 short coffee table book *The Way I Am*. The book is 208 pages, but most of those pages are photographs and lyric note sheets and other scrapbook mementos. Eminem called it "a scrapbook for fans."

Since Proof had died in 2006, Eminem was in desperate need of a replacement in his life and by his side. Mr. Porter stepped into those shoes as his hype man and the person he was in the studio most with. The other person who helped fill the void as a friend and co-collaborator music-wise was one-time enemy Royce Da.

Other extremely important friendships in Eminem's life include his enduring friendship with Kim, despite their tumultuous ups and downs and his relationships with Dre and Paul Rosenburg.

The story of how Eminem met Dre and started that friendship is somewhat well known.

A lesser-known friend of Eminem's is Wendy Day, an entrepreneur and huge rap fan who started a not-for-profit organization *Rap Coalition*, an organization that helps negotiate deals for hip-hop artists.

Day was an advocate for rappers who were getting horribly ripped off by America's biggest entertainment companies. Many were in debt and destitute, despite their records making billions of dollars of income for the companies. Because most of these rappers were African American these became known as "sharecropper deals" in a sad reference to black history in the immediate aftermath of slavery.

Day a white woman stepped in to change all that. Wendy Day's work, during the Golden Age of rap, helped make her and many of her clients multi-millionaires.

On the website *Genius.com*, Eminem has explained how Wendy Day helped make him who he is today.

Infinite had had only one good review. *Underground Soundz* said

> "His mastery of the English language allows him to write coherent stories, not just freestyle ramblings that happen to rhyme."

But no one paid that much attention to Marshall until he created Slim Shady.

Slim Shady scored a mention in *Source* magazine's unsigned hype column, and the pressing up of the *Slim Shady EP* was able to catapult him to local stardom in the Detroit scene overnight.

An EP is an extended play record, that contains more tracks than a single, but is unqualified as an album or LP. This was his demo and not the *Slim Shady LP* he later made with Dre.

Wendy Day heard the EP and called Marshall she said, "I want you to be on the battle team. I got you a ticket to the *Rap Olympics* in LA."

The Rap Olympics was held in 1997 in Los Angeles near LAX airport. The winner of the event would receive $500 and a Rolex watch.

Eminem explains further on the website *Genius*

> "I went to the *Olympics*, got all the way to the end, and then lost to the last guy.
>
> The guy who won was Otherwize, from LA. It was a local thing. They had a bunch of crowd support there. When I rapped, he went and hid behind a video screen. He walked away while I was rapping. I didn't have anyone to battle! I'd never been in a situation like that before. I went through a lot of people to get through to

the end, and then he walked away while I was rapping. I'm like, 'What the fuck do I do?' I was devastated.

I come off stage. I'm like, 'that's it. It's over for me.' This kid from *Interscope*, Dean Geistlinger, walks over, and he asks me for a copy of the CD. So, I kind of just chuck it at him. It was The Slim Shady EP. We come back to Detroit, I have no fucking home, no idea what I'm gonna do. Then, a couple weeks later, we get a call. Marky Bass said, 'Yo, we got a call from a doctor!'"

Eminem finally realized that Marky meant Dre, he started shouting, "don't you to me, man" multiple times.

Marshall planned to dress so Dre wouldn't forget him. Dre tells of how Eminem turned up in a "banana yellow" sweatshirt, bright yellow shoes. Dre said "everything he's wearing was bright yellow, and I'm like 'Damn!'"

Another long-time close friend is longtime manager Paul Rosenberg. Rosenberg was a kid the same age as Eminem. Paul was obsessed with rap and wanting to join the music business once he finished law school.

He discovered Eminem at the Hip Hop Shop and made friends with him. Paul was impressed by Marshall from watching him in underground battles hosted by Proof and even more, impressed by some of the crowd's reactions to him. Paul told *Rolling Stone* how some of the audience would say, "It's over just give it to the white boy" and "he's cold man, he's cold" a compliment.

After listening to *Infinite*, Paul was convinced to become Eminem's manager. He has remained Marshall's manager ever since.

Eminem has said Paul was his ticket to the mainstream because even at a young age Paul had connections.

Just as Kim Scott Mathers is the villain of Debbie Mathers' book, Paul Rosenberg is the villain of Eminem's body guard's book *Shady Buizzeness*. According to Big Naz, Paul was incredibly stingy with his staff and even Proof and Marshall himself.

Rosenberg's had sharp business instincts. He knew how to keep his business in the black. Big Naz even claimed Paul kept a very tight rein on Eminem's own spending to keep him from blowing his money while high. Everything had to be done through Paul. But Marshall always trusted Paul's judgement and never became resentful.

Eminem and Elton John have shared a close friendship since first coming together for a duet of Eminem's song *"Stan"* at the 2001 Grammys.

After a dispute with Dido over money, Eminem was looking for someone else to perform *Stan* with. Marshall told MTV, "We were debating on whether I was going to perform (at) the Grammys or not. I was like, 'The only way I'll perform at the Grammys is with Elton John.' And I was saying it in kind of jest, thinking it would never happen."

Eminem was still at the stage of not realizing how big a star he was, and not realizing other huge stars might indeed want to perform with him. He had no idea it was a possibility that a legend who was on *Soul Train*, *American Bandstand*, and *MTV* when he was a kid and teen would actually perform with him.

Eminem told *MTV* in a 2004 interview

"I didn't know he was gay. I didn't know anything about his personal life. I didn't really care." However, when he found out, he said, "Being that he was gay and he had my back, I think it made a statement in itself saying that he understood where I was coming from."

In an interview with *Beats 1* host Zane Lowe, Elton John said, "For me, Eminem was never homophobic, I listened to the whole of the Marshall Mathers album when I drove to a show in South Hampton, and I was floored by it. And I thought how could anyone think this is…he's just writing about the way things are. Not how he thinks, but the way things are."

Before the 2001 Grammy Awards, Eminem's four nominations triggered a storm of protest from activist groups such as the Gay and Lesbian Alliance Against Defamation (GLAAD), which released a statement saying that it was "appalled that John would share the stage with Eminem, whose words and actions promote hate and violence."

Elton John defended himself to the Los Angeles Times, stating that he would "rather tear down walls between people than build them up. If I thought for one minute that he was hateful, I wouldn't do it."

Eminem told MTV "The idea of it started becoming more, 'OK, this is a way to really flip it around and really f--- people's heads up.'"

Marshall mentions he had some concerns about the performance in his 2003 song *Business*.

You can even call collect, the most feared duet. Since me and Elton played career Russian Roulette And never even see me blink or get to bustin' a sweat

But the performance didn't do either star any damage.

Cynical activists commented that *The Grammys* like to bridge gaps for capitalistic reasons. It made sense that crossing hip-hop's biggest superstar and one of pop music's biggest stars would garner more viewership from each artists' fans.

Eminem rep Dennis Dennehy defended the duet to *Entertainment Weekly* at the time, insisting that Eminem wasn't just trying to polish his public image. "Regardless of what people are saying, Elton's been one of the more vocal artistic supporters of Eminem. He's said nothing but nice things about Eminem."

Eminem took home three Grammys out of four nominations that night in 2001, but it was his duet with John (they embraced after the song and held up their hands together in solidarity) that became the moment everyone was talking about the next day.

"It was more so just a statement, period," the rapper said in 2001. "If you really think that about me, you really don't know Marshall. You really don't know me."

Elton John interviewed Eminem in 2017 to help him promote his 2017 album *Revival*. In this *Interview Magazine* interview, Sir Elton talks about the first time he saw Eminem perform live:

"I was just mesmerized by you and your performance; it made the hairs on the back of my arms stand up. It was like seeing Mick Jagger for the first time. I hadn't really been exposed to that kind of rap in live performance before, and it was electrifying. And when that shit was thrown at you—about you being homophobic—I just thought, "I'm not standing for this. It's nonsense." I had to stand up and defend you. That Grammy performance was the start of a lovely friendship, and I'm grateful for that."

Elton John told *Rolling Stone,* "When David (Furnish) and I had our civil partnership, he sent us a present. In a case, on velvet cushions, were two diamond-studded cock rings. He gave us sex toys. So, there's a homophobe for you."

Eminem has mentioned Elton in a few songs. In his 2002 song, *My Dad's Gone Crazy*

Fuckin' brains, brawn, and brass balls, I cut'em off
And got 'em pickled and bronzed in a glass jar inside of a hall
With my framed autographed sunglasses with Elton John's name on my drag wall
I'm out the closet, I've been lyin' my ass off
All this time me and Dre been fuckin' with hats off (Suck it, Marshall)
So, tell Laura and her husband to back off
Before I push this motherfuckin' button and blast off

In his 2010 song, *Cold Wind Blows*

"Shawty dance while I dis you to the beat, fuck the words
You don't listen to 'em anyway, yeah struck a nerve sucker
Motherfucker might as well let my lips pucker
Like Elton John, cause I'm just a mean cock sucker."

Maybe the lines are a bit too focused on John's sexuality,

but then again, Eminem's lyrics often center on sex and the vulgar in general no matter who they are about. *Cold Wind Blows* is like *Criminal* and *Kill You* in that those songs were written very deliberately to be extremely offensive to make fun of the haters. *Cold Wind Blows* ends with God finally striking Marshall by lightening for saying so many offensive things.

In *Interview* magazine (Founded in 1969 by artist Andy Warhol.) Elton, John, interviewed Eminem. They greeted each other as follows

ELTON JOHN:" Hi, Marshall."
EMINEM: "How are you doing, cunt?"
JOHN: "I'm very well, you old bastard. Are you in
   Detroit?"
EMINEM: (laughs) "Yeah."

This is the way the two typically greet each other, Eminem enjoying the vulgar British greeting that is much more shocking in the USA than in Commonwealth countries. And enjoying the British humor of men calling each other that, which is not usually done in the USA.

Since the *Stan* performance, the two have become not just casual friends, but close friends who take a sincere interest in each other's lives and careers.

The deepest level of their friendship, though, is the way the two have bonded over their past histories with addiction.

There's little question Eminem did some drugs before he became seriously famous, but it was occasional, he probably rapped about illegal drugs more than he did them. After the happy, positive, upbeat *Infinite* album flopped and Eminem created the Slim Shady character, there were a lot of lyrics about drugs because Slim Shady did everything bad such as killing, raping people, and taking drugs. The early song *My Fault* is about mushrooms. But Eminem was probably not an addict at that stage.

In an interview with Music 360, Marshall discussed the drugs and the *Marshall Mathers LP*

"A couple of the songs on the new record were written on X. It exaggerates shit. Somebody will be just looking at me wrong, and I'll just flip a table over, like, 'what the fuck are you staring at?!' If you're in a good mood you love everybody, but if you're in a bad mood and you got shit on your mind, you're gonna break down and shit. The hardest shit that I've fucked with is X and 'shrooms."

This behavior possibly led to a lawsuit in which Miad Jarbou claimed he was beaten by Eminem at *Cheetah's on the Strip Gentlemen's Club*.

Jarbou said he was doing his business at a urinal when Eminem walked in and started doing the same. Jarbou claimed his friend entered the room and said: "Hey Eminem, what's up, man?" Marshall's bodyguard then said, "Shut the fuck up, man! Don't say another word." That's when Jarbou claims he said, "Hey man, my friend ain't starting trouble, it's just cool to see Eminem" at which time he says Eminem "stepped back from the urinal and without warning or provocation, as Jarbou continued to urinate, drove his fist in a violent punching manner into the side of Jarbou's face, knocking him to the ground."

Since Eminem cannot remember much of 2006, it is possible that this actually happened. The parallel between this and the time D'Angelo Baily beat Marshall at the urinal when he was just a ten-year-old kid at school is also striking.

Oddly, however, Jarbou waited over two years to file his lawsuit, filing it just as the statute of limitations was about to expire. Eminem's lawyers quickly had the suit dismissed.

Eminem has also hinted in songs that his problems may have started early in life with his mother encouraging him to take her prescription drugs to sedate him.

But in interviews, Eminem often blames the start of his addiction on the stress of touring. A person he describes as "well-meaning" gave him Ambien, which permitted him to get to sleep quickly, and so make more efficient use of his time while on tour.

The fact Ambien helped him sleep excited him and led him to seek other medication to help him cope with the stress of his occupation. He began mixing pills, adding Valium, Ambien, and Xanax to the mix, which led him to have very fuzzy memories of several years of his life to this day.

Just like his mother, he initially refused to believe friends who told him he had a drug problem because the only drugs he was using were prescribed.

Still, he tried going to rehab in 2005; his heart not in it and ordinary rehab was far from beneficial for him. Eminem told an interviewer at the BBC

> "I felt like Bugs Bunny in rehab. When Bugs Bunny walks into rehab, people are going to turn and look. People at rehab were stealing my hats and pens and notebooks and asking for autographs. I couldn't concentrate on my problem."

He relapsed shortly after causing Kim to find pills in his bedroom, leading to a fight with Kim that led to Kim telling him that she and the kids would not be in his *When I'm Gone* music video, leading to hired actors portraying Kim, Hailie, and Whitney in the final video.

To *Rolling Stone* Eminem said

"I got up to between 220 and 230, about 80 pounds heavier than I am now. I was going to McDonald's and Taco Bell every day. The kids behind the counter knew me – it wouldn't even faze them.

Or I'd sit up at Denny's or Big Boy and just eat by myself. It was sad. I got so heavy that people started to not recognize me. I remember being somewhere and overhearing these kids talking. One of them said, 'That's Eminem,' and the other said, 'No, it's not, man – Eminem ain't fat.' I was like, 'Motherfucker.' That's when I knew I was getting heavy."

His mother, Debbie Mathers, told the media she knew Eminem's weight gain was caused by the April 2006 death of Proof, and she was worried about his high blood pressure and high cholesterol. She claimed was ordering expensive "artery-clogging" filet minion steak most nights from a posh restaurant near to his mansion.

Debbie was quoted as saying that since Proof had died, "He's let his blond hair grow out, so everything but the ends are dark, his face has broken out in pimples, and he's put on so much weight that he's causing all sorts of other health problems for himself."

For once, Debbie was *proven* both truthful and correct.

Eminem, during an interview with Zane Lowe on *Radio 1*, claimed that at one point, he was taking up to 60 Valium and 30 Vicodin each day. He claimed Ambien knocked five years off his life.

After overdosing on methadone in December 2007, Marshall finally got the wakeup call. Looking at his daughters' faces, the hospital led him to finally get serious. At this point, he turned to Elton John for advice. Elton told him that he needed someone as famous as himself to be his sobriety coach, and Elton took on the new role enthusiastically.

Eminem stopped going to church rehab groups because people asked for his autograph, which made him shut down. Instead, he told *Rolling Stone* that under Elton's advisement he employed a professional rehab counselor whom he saw once a week, as well as his regular phone calls with Elton and he replaced his addiction to medications with an addiction to running and working out in order to lose the weight he had gained.

Of Elton John, as a sobriety coach, Eminem told *Rolling Stone*

"He was actually one of the first people I called when I wanted to get clean. He was hipping me to things, like, 'You're going to see nature that you never noticed before.' Shit you'd normally think was corny but that you haven't seen in so long that you just go, 'Wow! Look at that fucking rainbow!' Or even little things – trees, the color of leaves. I fucking love leaves now, man. I feel like I've been neglecting leaves for a long time."

In *Interview Magazine,* Eminem said to Elton John, "Getting clean made me grow up. I feel like all the years that I was using, I wasn't growing as a person."

Elton John said, "Me, too. If I had to go through that to get where I am now, then I'm very, very grateful. But I just can't believe I did some of that shit."

When asked what his sobriety date was, Eminem said: "4/20 ironically."

In *Interview Magazine,* Elton John said, "Your sobriety day is in my diary. I'm so proud of you. I'm 27 years clean, and when you get clean, you see things in a different way. It makes your life so much more manageable. It seems to have made all the difference—I can tell when I speak to you."

Elton ended the interview by saying, "I'm so happy you exist in the world, and I'm just so proud of you. You've worked so hard on yourself, and no one deserves this more than you, Marshall, and I love you from a long way away, okay?"

Eminem responded, "Thank you, Elton. I love you, too."

CHAPTER EIGHT

My rhymin' skills got you climbin' hills
I travel through your mind and to your spine like siren drills

---

Eminem's Process

(*I write songs for me, fuck what you like.*)

EMINEM HAD THIS TO SAY ABOUT HIS PROCESS TO *ROLLING Stone*. "I think the beat should talk to you and tell you what the hook is. The hook for *Just Lose It*- I probably wrote in about 30 seconds once the beat came on.

It was the last track we made for the album. We didn't feel like we had a single yet. That was a song that doesn't really mean anything. It's just what the beat was telling me to do.

To *Spin* magazine, in 2004, Dr. Dre said, "Not only does he not know how to work a computer, he refuses to learn."

Eminem said, "If I learn how to work a computer, I'm

going to be on that bitch all day looking at comments about me, and it's going to drive me crazy."

Paul Rosenberg, his manager, said, "anytime he reads a blog or a review about himself, it affects him for a long time."

Eminem's aversion to computers and the internet clearly changed in 2015, though, when Eminem became an investor, on the website Genius, and began commenting on lyrics on the site.

To *Rolling Stone*, Eminem claimed that the only book he'd ever read cover to cover, more than once, was LL Cool J's *I Make My Own Rules*. A big LL fan, Eminem, claimed the 1998 autobiography is the only book he's read that wasn't just read to him as a child. *The Little Engine That Could* was a favorite in that category.

Another children's book Marshall has said that he loved as a kid was *The Ugly Duckling*. One can only speculate whether it was Debbie, or his much loved Aunt Edna, that read these books to him.

But Marshall also claimed in other interviews that the only book he had ever read was the dictionary, which he consults all the time for rhymes.

Eminem may have been joking about only reading the dictionary and only reading one autobiography.

At times you have to take things Eminem says in interviews with a grain of salt. For example, Eminem was clearly only joking with some things he's said to interviewers such as the lie that he was on Tinder and Grindr, and the lie that he hits himself in the head with a hammer to put himself to sleep at night. He also once lied to an interviewer claiming he was gay just to get a reaction.

To *CNN's* Anderson Cooper, Eminem was possibly more honest. He said, "I found that no matter how bad I was at school, and no matter how low my grades might have been sometimes, I was good at English, always good at English ... I just felt like I wanna be able to have all of these words at my disposal, in my vocabulary at all times whenever I need to pull 'em out. You know, somewhere, they'll be stored, like, locked away."

Rumor has it, though, that the reason he failed the ninth grade was because he spent all year making love to Kim.

To Anderson Cooper, Marshall also said: "I was beat up in the bathrooms, in the hallways, shoved in the lockers." I found something.. 'yeah, this kid over here may have more chicks or better clothes, but he can't do this like me, I started to feel like, 'Maybe Marshall is getting a little respect.'"

Eminem has admitted many of his songs written for his second through fourth album were written while taking the club drug ecstasy.

As a result, he has a whole different version of arguably most famous song *Lose Yourself* from the *8 Mile* Soundtrack, that he does not even remember writing a word of. This different version of *Lose Yourself* includes lines like

> *If I was froze inside of a moment*
> *If I could capture time inside a capsule, an hourglass full*
> *Of sand in the palm of my hand, it passes through it*
> *If I can grasp it and just control what happens to it*
> *Then I can trap it, so no more time elapses through it*
> *If raps could do it, maybe I could tap into it*
> *Then I could try to channel it through Cadillacs and Buicks*

And

> *'Cause when we descend together, we begin to move as one*
> *In perfect unison just like the moon and sun*

Eminem has said because of drugs, he, unfortunately, doesn't remember writing this song at all.

"The pills had a lot to do with it. Just wiping out brain cells. I don't know if it sounds like I'm making excuses, but the absolute truth is a lot of my memory is gone. I don't know if you've ever taken Ambien, but it's kind of a memory-eraser. That s**t wiped out five years of my life.

"People will tell me stories, and it's like, 'I did that?' I saw myself doing this thing on (TV network) *BET* recently, and I was like, 'When was that?'

To Elton John who interviewed him for *Interview* Magazine, he said

---

> "With every song, all the elements have to work. First, the beat has to be great—you start there. You start with the music, and then the ideas follow. Then you start thinking of rhymes, and then you record it, and sometimes—this happens to me a lot—it doesn't come out as good as it did in my head when I first wrote it."

In the interview, Elton John commiserated, "It's so frustrating when that happens. I fucking hate it!"

Eminem has different modes, intense raw autobiography, wildly offensive horrorcore, political songs, and songs romanticizing bad relationship and domestic violence recorded with immensely talented female singers such as *Love the Way You Lie, Tragic Endings, Need Me.*

The domestic violence songs may be troubling, but are perhaps, just Eminem's reluctance to be cliché with a love song.)

Other Eminem staples include powerful, motivational songs like *Lose Yourself*, *'Til I Collapse*, *Guts Over Fear*, *Beautiful* and *Not Afraid*, and purely comedic songs like *My Band* and *Heat*. His comedy songs often have cheesy joke lines, puns, and hooks that are less sonically appealing. But the public is lucky that Eminem gives his audience so many different vibes.

People have claimed that *Revival* had no theme, but it could be argued that *Revival's* theme was a kind of showcase in which Eminem gave a little taste of what all different kinds of people enjoyed about his past work. In his interview with Elton John for *Interview* Magazine, Eminem explained, "The album is called *Revival*. It's a reflection of where I'm at right now, but also, I feel like what I tried to do was diversify. I've tried to make a little something for everyone."

Podcaster Malcolm Gladwell had Eminem as a guest on his show. To Gladwell, Marshall said, "My first rhyme for rap was written at my Aunt Edna's house. It was so much of LL (Cool J)."

Eminem then goes on to mention to Gladwell, that he struggled with writing the lyrics for *Revival*. "When you start out in your career, you have a blank canvas. And then your second album comes out, and you paint a little more, and you paint a little more, by the time you get to your seventh and eighth album, you've already painted all over it. There's nowhere else to paint."

Eminem, in his famous 2018 *Sway* interview, explains how the mistakes he made with *Relapse,* helped him create the massively successful *Recovery* album of 2010.

Likewise, all the trashing by critics and Trump fans of his

21017 album *Revival* led to the lyrics of 2018s *Kamikaze* which claps back at his critics using the popular trap beats of the modern age.

Ice-T once quoted Dr. Dre in *Rolling Stone* as saying, "You've gotta write me a song. I don't need bars — I know you've got skills, but we need songs, so give me the hook first." Ice Tea went on to say "A lot of rappers get lost, but that's what Eminem does. They write these incredible songs, and that's basically what Dre likes to take to the marketplace."

In other words, Dre and Eminem focus on finding their standout hooks first, before Eminem plugs in his previously written bars, and that's how the two of them have been able to create such powerful songs.

Eminem has spent most of his life working nine to five since his teenage years. The one big exception being when he decided to use his savings and investments to live on for much of four years while he got clean and sober and spent time with Hailie and his other kids.

Rapper Akon told a story about working on the song "Smack That with Eminem.

Akon said, "Like he comes in at nine am every day to the studio, takes his lunch break at one. And he's out of there about five pm."

Akon went on to say, "Eminem is the first artist that I worked with that actually treated the business like a real job. I didn't expect him to be like that. I turned up at his studio at six pm thinking we'd have a late-night studio session.

But Em just left. (I rang and said) 'Em where you at?' He said, 'I'm outta here!' I said, 'I just got here, you comin' back?' He said, 'Yeah, I'll be back there at nine am.' I said, 'you're joking, right?' he said, 'Nah, nah, I'm serious. I'll see you at nine. You don't get up early?' I said, 'yeah yeah, I'll be there.' He goes, takes his lunch, hour come back

So, I get back there at nine, and he shows up on time. (We) play some beats we robin, we rockin', so I'm in the middle of writing a record. He's like, "we about to go out for lunch.' I said alright, cool, I'll meet you after.' He said, 'You're not gonna take no lunch?' I said, 'No, no, I'm not hungry. I'm still at work.' He's like 'alright cool, 'he goes, takes his lunch, hour come back, he's back (says) 'What we got?'

I play him the record, play him the chorus. He's like, 'Oh, this is it! Boom.' He goes into this verse...five o'clock comes, he halfway in. He's like 'alright bro I'm gonna see you tomorrow.'

So, at this point, I'm like 'yo but your verse almost done you ain't gonna finish it?' He's like 'No, no, I'm gonna finish it tomorrow. So, at this point, I'm like 'Yo, this is crazy, right?'

So tomorrow comes, he's like... he finishes up. So...I asked him I was like 'yo what's up with the work ethic?' He's like 'Nah, man, you know? I just like to be here. I treat it like a real job. I don't make it no more than what it's supposed to be. I don't allow it to stress me out. Stay as long as I have to. I got a family. I got daughters. I wanna spend time with 'em. I wanna make time.'"

Akon goes on to say, "And I stopped, and I said, "Damn, you know what he's right! Cause sometimes I'll be in the studio, three, four days don't come out. Don't see my kids, don't call my wife. None of that. I'm just like working! You know what I'm saying? And I'm sitting there like 'Man that makes a lot of sense because ain't nothing going to change between today and tomorrow.'"

At this point, host Navjosk, founder of hiphop-n-more.-

com, interjects to say, "And you're rich either way. You can come back tomorrow. It makes no difference." Akon responds, "Exactly, like nothing gonna change. We're creating, right? So, what's the rush?"

In an interview with *Montreality*, Atlanta-based rapper TI, said "Eminem is probably one of the most talented, capable, intellectual technicians of wordplay I have ever experienced. "He's really meticulous with his approach to how he put his shit together. Both times we worked together I had the opportunity to sit in there and watching him actually put this shit together, it was just truly of another world. For real, that shit was just on some other shit.

He and Andre3000 are the most meticulous artists I have ever worked with, and they are very critical of themselves. There were times where I felt shit was dope, and they were like, 'Naw.'"

T.I., who worked with Eminem in 2007 on *T.I. vs. T.I.P.* track *Touchdown* and again in 2010 on *No Mercy* highlight, *That's All She Wrote*.

In *Something From Nothing: The Art of Rap,* a 2012 American documentary, directed and executive produced by Ice-T, Eminem explains more of his process.

"My mind 24/7 is thinking about ways to bend words" into rhymes."

Few musicians are as qualified as Ice-T to direct a documentary on the accomplishments of classic rap artists. In the film, Eminem hangs out with the famous gangsta rapper. They openly discuss Eminem's battle with drugs. "Without rap, I wouldn't be here," Marshall admits.

> "Who would have thought that one of the greatest rappers of all time would be a white cat?" Ice-T responds.

In the film, the two explore Eminem's process of writing, explaining that this involves, rhyming as many lyrics as he can come up within each bar of music.

In a 2007 interview with *Complex Magazine*, Eminem discussed his process as a producer. Eminem explained that his mindset was that there was no point in working for two hours on a beat if no one was going to pick it, so he often started with a skeleton beat, a technique he learned from Dre. Both Dre and Eminem like to start with a skeleton beat and then add more shape once someone lays a verse.

Marshall felt 50 Cent didn't really get it at first back in 2002 and wasn't very impressed with the skeleton beat Eminem had sent him for the song *Patiently Waiting*.

Eminem said he kept calling 50, saying, "Did you write to that yet? Please write to that! I'm telling you that could be crazy! And all 50 heard was just the drums. And then when he put a verse to the chorus…he came to Detroit, and he played it for me…and he had a hook, two verses…and I knew that was the track that I wanted to get on and as soon as I heard the track and the way like…the chorus was smooth, and then it got aggressive like

'*I've been patiently waiting I been patiently waitin'*
 for a
track to explode on
You can stunt if you want and yo.'
Ass 'll get rolled on.'

And I was like 'Oh Shit!' Like I didn't even hear that. I didn't even hear that melody in that beat. I don't know how the fuck he pulled that melody out of that beat. But he did, and I was like OK .... now we can add more music, and.... that was the craziest song that me and 50 did together.

Marshall goes on to explain in the interview that 50 was on deadline for the release of his 2003 album Get Rich or Die Tryin' and that they never got to be in the studio together. Eminem also said he would have added more music to the song if they'd had more time.

According to popular Youtuber, *The Pop Song Professor,* real name Clifford Stumme. Eminem's most popular songs are, on average, 645 words long, and on average, the stanzas are, on average, 1.24 syllables per word if you include all the one-syllable words. Stumme says he spent ten hours counting, quantifying, comparing, and averaging 32 Eminem songs to find these results.

The Pop Song Professor compares Eminem to Kayne, pointing out that one of Kayne's most popular songs has fewer syllables per word.

According to the Guinness Book of World Records, Eminem's *Rap God* set a new world record for most words in a song with Marshall Mathers working his way through 1,560 words in 6'04", at an average of 4.28 words per second.

In Eminem's songs, multiple stanzas will all correlate with some type of rhyme, and he does that by constantly brainstorming and writing down (often on napkins or whatever is handy) thousands of rhymes that he later works into some type of song.

Eminem is commonly known for connecting the same sound several times in a row, often using the poetry technique of assonance. Assonance is the resemblance of sound between syllables of nearby words, arising mainly from the rhyming of two or more stressed vowels, but not consonants.

One example of assonance is the line from Eminem's 2004 song *Yellow Brick Road*. In the song, Eminem talks about meeting his late best friend and former hype man for the first time.

> *I told him to stop by and check us out sometime*
> *He looked at me like I'm out my mind*
> *Shook his head, like, "White boys don't know how to rhyme."*
> *I spit out a line and rhymed "birthday" with "first place."*
> *And we both had the same rhymes that sound alike*

Eminem has also mentioned this in his brief 2008 autobiography, saying that he and Proof, when they met at ages sixteen and fifteen, found that they had both rhymed birthday with first place. This "rhyme" is an example of assonance rhyming.

Another interesting fact from Stumme is that Eminem's *Revival* used only slightly less foul language than his most popular and famous songs. Revival had 2.07 swear words per 100 words compared to 2.08 swear words per 100 words in Eminem's older classics.

On of Stumme's most interesting revelations about Eminem's writing is that the Revival album had 41% "sad toned" songs compared to Eminem's most popular longs, which were predominately "anger toned" at 60%. This could undoubtedly account in part for negative reactions to *Revival*.

Stumme has not analyzed Kamikaze in the same way, but it's fair to say Eminem went back to anger rather than the sad songs that many people objected to on *Revival*. On Revival

Eminem expressed his insecurities on *Walk on Water*, mourned bad relationships and songs like *Tragic Endings*, *Need Me* and *Bad Husband*, and mourned problems in his country such as gun violence and mass shootings in the song *Nowhere Fast*, police brutality to African Americans on *Untouchable* and the deficiencies in Trump's leadership on *Like Home*. The amount of depressing content on the album was maybe too much for some listeners. But mature Eminem was dealing with important concepts.

Castle and *Arose* are also sad songs reflecting on his near-death experience in 2007 when he overdosed on methadone. So, while the whole album was not bitter, the majority of songs had a sad tone.

Autobiographical songs like *Castle* and *Arose* are more appreciated by fans than a song like Walk on Water that exposed his insecurities as a rapper, and male fans tend to slam the relationship songs with female singers on the hooks, while women buy the songs in bulk catapulting *Love the Way You Lie* to the top of the charts and making it one of Eminem's most successful songs in terms of sales.

CHAPTER NINE

Kick back,
While I kick facts, yeah, Dre—
sick track
Perfect way to get back

———

Eminem and his Beefs
(*Michael Jackson is extremely upset.*)

EMINEM'S LINGUISTIC GLADIATOR BATTLES HAVE LONG fascinated some of the public. It's well known that Eminem came up through battle rap, battling at the Detroit *Hip-hop Shop,* and Eminem increased the public's knowledge of battle rap with his involvement in the movie *8 Mile.*

Though the days of battling one on one are long gone for Mathers, Eminem has always been part of the hip-hop trend to hit back at enemies in songs.

This book has already covered some of his most famous beefs, such as his beef with ICP and Joe Budden, Tyler the

Creator, and Earl Sweatshirt. As well as his love life "beefs" with Mariah Carey and Kim and his political beefs with Bush and Trump.

The following are some of his other beefs that caught the interest of the public.

Michael Jackson

In 2002 one of Michael Jackson's most notorious moments was when he dangled his baby Blanket over the balcony of a German hotel. Jackson told the press that he had been doing something kind. "It was a kind act. Showing the fans, the baby." A lot of the public and the press didn't see it that way feeling that in that moment, the baby had been had risk. Sweden magazine *Expressen* featured the headline *Jackson plays with the baby's life*. The Sun headline was *You Lunatic,* while the UK's *Daily Mirror's* headline was *Mad Bad Dad.*

Jackson later apologized via his lawyer calling it a "terrible mistake" "I got caught up in the excitement of the moment. I would never intentionally endanger the lives of my children."

In 2003 Eminem surprised fans in Glasgow Scotland by appearing at a window wearing a surgical mask and holding a blond baby. Some onlookers, unaware of the ages of Eminem's children, screamed in fear. One or two screamed "Hailie," apparently unaware that Hailie was seven at the time.

Spoofing Jackson's infamous baby-dangling incident Eminem actually tossed his "baby" up in the air. It turned out to be a blond doll.

Michael Jackson reportedly laughed off the incident. A

source close to the singer told his Belgium "Billie Jean" fan club. "Michael thinks things like this are hilarious; he has a very good sense of humor."

However, in 2004, Jackson was not amused by the lyrics and video for the song "Just Lose It."

Come here little kiddies, on my lap
Guess who's back with a brand new rap
And I don't mean rap
As in a new case of child molestation accusation
No worries, papa's got a brand new bag of toys
What else could I possibly do to make noise
I done touched on everything, but little boys
And that's not a stab at Michael
That's just a metaphor I'm just psycho

In a Fox News exclusive, Michael Jackson said, "I've never met Mr. Eminem. I've always admired him, and to have him do something like that was pretty painful as an artist to another artist, and it's sad because I think what Stevie Wonder said is true, and I don't want to say too much more than that. He should be ashamed of himself…. I've been an artist, most of my life….and I've never attacked another fellow artist. Great artists don't do that."

Stevie Wonder said to *Billboard* magazine: "Kicking someone when he's down is not a good thing. (referring to child molestation charges that had been recently leveled at Jackson for the second time by Gavin Arvizo.) I was disappointed that he would let himself go to such a level. Eminem has succeeded on the backs of people predominately in that lower pay bracket, people of color. So far for him to come out like that is bullshit." Both Stevie Wonder and Jackson tried to hint that the spoof was racist.

While interviewing Eminem in 2004, Sway Calloway remarked, "In the past, you could say certain things about certain artists, now when you make a song called *Just Lose It,* you become a target, and I know Michael Jackson has spoken out against your video. Marshall responded by covering his mouth to stop a laugh, then said, "That was never intended to be anything more than just spoofing pop icons from the 80s. As far as his music, the man is a legend. As far as his personal business, I'm neither here nor there with it."

While the Just Lose it Video makes fun of Madonna and PeeWee Herman, Jackson is spoofed the most with the video showing kids jumping on Jackson's bed, Jackson's nose falling off, Jackson's hair catching on fire (referencing his accident during the Pepsi ad and putting the fire out by sticking his head in the toilet and also Eminem profusely vomiting all over Jackson.

In another interview, Eminem said he was surprised by Michael Jackson's reaction to the song and video. "The parodies have been the jumpstart of my career that launched me with *My Name Is.* In the third verse, I make fun of myself."

Some people have pointed out however the one moment when Eminem vomits profuse green vomit all over Michael Jackson in the video would hint that Eminem believed Jackson was a child molester although Eminem was very careful to claim he had no opinion just as Sean Lennon claimed the same despite the video for his song Bubble's Burst also largely hinting that Lennon supported the alleged victims of Michael Jackson.

Michael Jackson then seemed to get even madder. "I am very angry at Eminem's depiction of me in his video," Jackson said in an interview with a Los Angeles radio station. "I feel that it is outrageous and disrespectful. It is one thing to spoof, but it is another to be demeaning and insensitive. The video was inappropriate and disrespectful to me, my children, my family, and the community at large."

Eminem responded in an MTV interview, "Michael Jackson sitting on the edge of a bed with little kids jumping on the bed? That aint nothing that he didn't admit to doing or tell us himself he was doing."

One of Jackson's spokespeople then told reporters that legal action was being considered and called for channels to boycott the Just Lose It video. *Black Entertainment Television*, BET complied with Jackson's request and pulled the video.

Comedian George Carlin said during one of his routine's "I'm not fucking with Michael Jackson fans I'm not that dumb. Mike's sweet, his fans are vicious. Attack him; you're already considered dead." Eminem seemed aware of this in his interviews following the Just Lose It video.

To Sway, Eminem said, "I talk all the time in my songs about being chased by the paparazzi and people making fun of me 'cause they don't understand who I really am. And if there's anybody who has had it worse than me it's Michael Jackson, so that's one of the main reasons, I didn't come back with a diss song against Michael Jackson (after Michael dissed him in interviews.)

I mean, I mention the neverland ranch a few times, but I don't take it too far, plus, he's the biggest star on the planet. He's more famous than the president…and plus he has like (a-cajelion) fans around the world."

Sway said I can't picture you listening to Michael Jackson in your room going "hee-hee."

Eminem bursts out laughing but then says, "Nah seriously when *Thriller* came out, I was the first one on my block who bought the album…this guy is a freaking genius, and I idolize the way he performs, and that's that."

Jackson did not end up suing Eminem for the song and video. However, despite Eminem's apologies for offending Jackson, some people felt Jackson got his revenge in 2007 when Michael Jackson's partnership company *Sony/ATV* purchased the publishing company *Famous Music* for $370 million. The deal gave Sony and Michael Jackson the rights to over 125,000 songs, of which Eminem's songs were the most high-profile and the most profitable. The deal included the songs *Without Me* and *The Real Slim Shady*.

INSANE CLOWN POSSE

How the ICP beef started is a funny story. In 1996 ICP was huge, and Eminem was barely known. Marshall was throwing a record release party at St. Andrew's Hall for his first album Infinite. Marshall's sneaky attempt to get Detroit hip hop and horrorcore fans to come to the record release party of an unknown rapper was to put the names of Detroit superstars on his flyer with the word "maybe" in brackets after their name.

Violent J of ICP caught wind of Eminem's promotional stunt and was none too pleased the upstart rapper was using ICP - and a nonexistent ICP performance - to drum up interest and publicity for himself. Violent J heard about this and said, "Nah, we don't know him. We ain't fuckin doin' that".

Violent J confronted Marshall about the flyer, and Eminem said pleasantly, "well, the flyer is an invite I'm inviting you now." Violent J's response was, "F*ck no, I ain't coming to your party. We might have, if you would've asked us first, before putting us on the fuckin' flyer like this."

They were later to regret blowing him off. The seed was sown for a years-long feud.

During the same month that Eminem pulled a gun on John Guerra, he also flashed his 9mm pistol outside a car audio shop during an argument with an associate of rival rap group, *Insane Clown Posse*. The prosecutor in the Warren case sought at least a six-month prison sentence, but as in the Guerra case, expensive lawyers managed to get Marshall a sentence of probation only. After losing Proof, Eminem changed his tune about guns and in 2017, even wrote an anti-NRA song called *Nowhere Fast*.

Stating:

They love their guns more than our children
Shhh, think another one just entered in our buildin'

Canibus

Canibus' beef with Eminem started in. In the early '90s, Eminem and Canibus shared many similarities as they both made some waves in the underground scene. Eminem praised Canibus to local Detroit media.

In an interview on Tim Westwood's hip-hop show, Eminem explained that the beef started because Canibus approached him in 1998 and asked if Marshall ghost-wrote the lyrics to LL Cool J's "The Ripper Strikes Back" which was a diss to Canibus.

Eminem denied it. But Canibus made it clear he didn't believe Marshall. The year was 1998, and Eminem was actually impressed by Canibus's talent, but the rapper (real name Germaine Williams) rebuffed him. Canibus would live to deeply regret this.

In 2002 Canibus wrote a track called *U Didn't Care* that was all about the character Stan from Eminem's huge hit

Stan. In the song, Canibus accuses Eminem of not caring about Stan's death. In his song, Stan doesn't die. He has been saved using an advanced form of genetic manipulation, using nanotechnology called extremis (mentioned in *Iron Man* comics) Stan talks to Eminem in his new form. He appears now as an MC who collaborates with another rapper.

The subject matter of the song is creative and original.

They showed me techniques to help me pressure
whenever I remember that crazy night when I was being reckless
Drivin with a death wish, on the bridge I crashed into a Lexus
Right before I finished that last sentence
I was listenin' to Xzibit's album "Restless."
The next thing I knew I was underwater and breathless
I was unconscious for a second, literally dying to go to heaven
'till some fellas came and pulled me from the wreckage

Canibus then used Stan in several other concept songs. Canibus was then lucky enough to be dissed in a couple of songs on 2002's *The Eminem Show*. One was *Square Dance*.

I'll be brief, and let me just keep shit simple
Can-I-Bitch don't want no beef with Slim, nooo!
Not even on my radar
So, won't you please jump off my dick, lay off, and stay off?
And follow me as I put these crayons to chaos
From séance to séance

Another was *Say What You Say*.

If you ever mix me up or confuse me
With a Canibus or Dre with a Dupri
We'll rub it in, every club you're in
We'll have you blackballed
And make sure you never rap a-fucking-gain

In 2003 Eminem also released a full diss track. In which he made fun of Canibus's album that went Gold and not Platinum.

His album came, and it was not good
I think it went lead or double copper-wood

Canibus was a great lyricist and very creative, but unfortunately, Canibus's career never reached great heights. The beef is thought to have hurt him.

Cage

One of Eminem's first-ever public beefs was with Cage. Cage is a rapper born in from Middletown, Orange County, New York, with the real name of Christian Palko.

In 1993 Cage was featured on a song by Pete Nice called *Rich Bring 'Em Back* on the album *Dust to Dust*. This was Cage's first big break working with a bigger name. On this song, Cage spat, "The misses gets a hysterectomy for disrespecting me."

Three years later, in 1996 on his album *Infinite* in his song *Open Mic* Eminem spat, "You bitches get a hysterectomy disrespectin' me."

Infinite as an album was panned for copying New York sound and New York rappers.

Of course, *Infinite* made so little impact with less than 500 copies sold that Cage was not even aware of the lines at the time.

However, Cage's schtick was always the crazy wild white boy from New York. When Eminem came on the scene, Cage saw his own rude, white boy schtick in Slim Shady. Wendy Day tried to get Cage to battle with Eminem, but Cage checked him out and found the hysterectomy line on *Infinite* and became enraged. Cage also seemed intimidated by all the hype surrounding Eminem in the scene.

As Eminem's star rose Cage began to tell the press that Eminem had copied his style and lyrics for his Slim Shady persona and well as copying him on the one lyric in *Infinite*. The music and beats on Infinite also had the real New York sound of the time that Cage used, but Cage and Eminem were both thought to have been influenced by AZ and Nas.

There is a myth that Cage once battled Eminem; however, Mathers told the press that every time Wendy Day and others tried to set up a battle between Eminem and Cage, that Cage never showed up.

Eminem "Every time I turned up to battle him, he wasn't there; he was never to be found."

Interviewer "This Cage kid wouldn't show?"

Eminem "Age kid let's not give him any more press than he deserves. We'll say Age or Rage or Stage or Gage whatever, whatever it doesn't matter, or H we'll say H like HIV."

Interviewer laughs.

Eminem certainly comes off better in interviews about the beef than Cage, who can only stumble, call Eminem, "Nigger," with a lot of umming and erring until finally, he states he felt the arranged battles were all somehow a "set up." And then Cage finally states it was proven a "set up" by the fact that Wendy Day was trying to get him to battle Eminem in 1997 and Eminem signed to Aftermath in 1998. Not really a very convincing or even understandable argument? What was a setup? A set up for Cage to fail unfairly in a battle? How would it have been unfairly set up against him? Cage doesn't explain.

Cage never battled Eminem, but once Eminem blew up, Cage used him as material many times. On the track *Escape to '88* Cage (like MGK) tries to claim Eminem had him blackballed. "Being blackballed by a white MC, pause, I guess that faggot found the right MD" in *Bitch Lady* Cage did a skit mocking Eminem's hit single *Just Don't Give A Fuck.*

Eminem responded in 1999 on a Sway & King Tech album *This or That* in the song *Get You Mad* "Went on stage and sprayed Cage wit Agent Orange And wiped my ass wit his page in Source."

Way before MGK, Cage was the first rapper to get some attention off the back of Eminem by writing an entire diss track about him. When *The Slim Shady LP* blew up in 1999, Cage, who had been too afraid to battle Eminem face to face, released the diss track *The Illest 4 Letter Word,* in which he promises to drown Eminem in Lake Michigan in an intro that doesn't even rhyme.

Later on, in the song, he spits, "Waste your little infant see you thinking different." In this line, Cage threatens to kill three-year-old Hailie. Cage was the first rapper to attempt to strike this low blow against Eminem, but unfortunately, not the last.

Everlast

Was the next rapper to try this pathetic stunt of picking on Eminem's little girl for the pettiest of reasons. Everlast believed that Eminem had ignored him backstage at a 1999 concert. In the year 2000 Everlast

Cock my hammer, spit a comet like Halley
I'll buck a .380 on ones that act Shady

Eminem was currently on the Anger Management Tour when he was notified of Everlast's insult.

Though the line is referencing Halley's Comet and is more intelligent and less nasty that Cage, this was the one Eminem chose to hit back at, possibly because Everlast had more cred than Cage or perhaps because Cage didn't mention his baby's name at all, calling her only "your infant."

Regardless Eminem really hit back at Everlast (aka Whitey Ford) mocking Everlast's career, his age and even his heart troubles in several songs including lines like

You a Black Jesus, heart attack, seizures
Too many cheeseburgers McDonald's Big Mac
    greasers
White devil washed up honkey
Mixed up cracker who crossed over to country

At the end of the diss track song, *Quitter* Eminem spits *Mention my daughter's name in a song again, you fucking punk Ayo!*

The record label, *Tommy Boy Records,* issued a statement

on behalf of Everlast, "He is amused. He thinks that the song is quite funny."

Limp Bizkit

Fred Durst and *Limp Bizkit* wanted to jump into the feud between Everlast and Eminem because the feud was making a big splash in the media.

Fred Durst approached Eminem, saying they wanted to do a collaboration with him to diss Everlast. Group member DJ Lethal also told Eminem that he "fucking hated" Everlast.

Eminem booked the studio time, and on the day they were supposed to record the track, Durst backed out with a toothache, while DJ Lethal said he was cool with Everlast now and didn't want to.

Marshall was fine with all of this and made the song by himself. But two weeks later Marshall was watching MTV, and DJ Lethal was talking smack about Marshall saying his former House of Pain group mate Everlast could whoop Eminem in a fight.

Eminem told the press, "I'm sitting back watching the TV like 'What? You were supposed to be on the song with me!' I would not have made a move if it wasn't for that. If 10-20 million people did not see him say that Everlast would whoop my ass. So that's why I dissed him…If you didn't want to be in the beef, you should've stayed out of it, you shouldn't have opened your mouth."

JA RULE

Ja Rule is known for making one of the nastiest disses to

Hailie that really made Eminem want to quit beefing altogether. Ja Rule released the diss track *Loose Change* in April 2003, where he attacks 50 Cent, as well as Eminem and Dr. Dre.

Eminem first got dragged into Ja Rule's ugly beef with 50 Cent, when he signed 50 to his *Shady Records* imprint in 2002.

What started as a local beef between two rappers from Queens, New York quickly turned into an all-out war between record labels. Ja Rule and his label *Murder Inc* battling with Interscope.

This was one of the most well-known feuds in hip-hop history. The FBI probed the label *Murder Inc's* ties to McGriff, who was allegedly involved in the murder of Jam Master Jay in 2002. This was never proven, and the murder of Jam Master Jay was unfortunately never solved.

According to the website *The Smoking Gun*, there was a search warrant affidavit for the label. The label *Murder Inc* was rumored at that time to have issues with money laundering and even assassination attempts on other rappers.

Eminem was only a minor player in the beef until Ja Rule's diss track "Loose Change" included the lyrics: "Em you claim your mother's a crack head, Kim's a known slut, so what's Hailie gonna be when she grows up?"

This, unfortunately, wasn't even the scariest Hailie diss, however.

Benzino

One of the most talked about feuds of the early 2000s began when Benzino gave The Marshall Mathers LP two stars out of five in his magazine *The Source*.

Benzino, real name Raymond Scott, tried desperately to make money off of Eminem fame, claiming that he birthed Marshall's career by featuring him in the Unsigned Hype column in *The Source* back in 1998.

This is something Eminem appeared to admit was accurate on his 2004 song *Like Toy Soldiers*

> *Some receptionist at The Source who answers phones at his desk*
> *Has an erection for me and thinks that I'll be his resurrection?*
> *Tries to blow the dust off his mic and make a new record*
> *But now he's fucked the game up 'cause one of the ways I came up*
> *Was through that publication, the same one that made me famous*
> *Now the owner of it has got a grudge against me for nothin'?*

50 cent hosted *Hot 97*, and Eminem called in to promote his movie *8 Mile* where he called his now enemy- "Hasbenzino."

Benzino released a few different Eminem diss tracks.

Eminem responded with *Nail in the Coffin,* and *The Sauce* Eminem criticized Benzino for using his son to boost his own record sales:

> *Here's a poster of Ray-Ray and his dad*
> *You wanna talk about some shit*
> *That you don't know about, yeah?*
> *Let's talk about how you're puttin' your own son out there*

> *To try to eat off him because you missed your boat*
> *You're never gonna blow, bitch, you're just too old*
> *No wonder you're sore now, lordy, you're bored now*
> In response in *Die Another Day Benzino* got scary
> *And you better keep my kids out ya fuckin' mouth*
> *Before I put a Glock in yo' motherfuckin' mouth*
> *Tell Hailie it ain't safe no more (nah)*
> *Daddy better watch yo' back at the candy store*
> *We fucked up, resort to plan B*
> *Fuck around she end up like JonBenét*

Later Benzino tried to damage Eminem's career when one of the members of *Soul Intent* sold him the track *Ole Foolish Pride*.

The disses from Ja Rule and Benzino respectively saying Hailie would grow up to be a drugged out promiscuous woman, and the actual death threat from Benzino appeared to be a bit much for Eminem.

Adding to his stress were the rumored links Ja Rule's label *Murder Inc* had to an actual, alleged murder. Not to mention the two alleged assignation attempts on Marshall's life by convicted felon, Bloods gang member and CEO of rap label *Death Row Records,* Suge Knight.

Though never charged by any prosecutor for any involvement, Suge Knight has been the subject of theories in popular culture about the unsolved murders of two well-known rap artists. Tupac Shakur and The Notorious B.I.G. (AKA Biggie Smalls.)

However, Cathy Scott, author of *The Killing of Tupac Shakur* and *The Murder of Biggie Smalls*, makes a sound argument that Knight would never have placed himself in the path of bullets he knew were coming. Suge was in the car with Tupac when Tupac was shot. And in 2018, another rapper confessed to killing Tupac.

Regardless while Suge was not a known murderer at the time of the alleged assassination attempts on Eminem, Suge has since been convicted of numerous crimes and in 2017 was convicted of the murder of film producer Terry Carter.

Suge Knight was furious that a film *Straight Outta Compton* was being made about Dre's rap group N.W.A. Dre had a restraining order against Suge, which he violated by turning up on the set.

Producer Terry Carter was described at his funeral as a man who was always trying to unite people despite their differences and keep the peace.

Tragically, it seems his efforts may have been a factor in his violent death. He tried to talk to Suge about making peace with the people surrounding Dre so he could collaborate with them in the future. Suge apparently furious with Carter for giving Dr. Dre even more fame deliberately ran Carter over with his car.

By 2004, Marshall was dealing with threats from Murder Inc, Death Row Records, and Suge Knight. He was upset about Ja Rule saying disgusting things about Hailie and Benzino, making death threats towards Hailie in a song.

This led to the viral 2004 song *Like Toy Soldiers* in which Eminem raps about how beefing had become too dangerous, and he was bowing out from it.

> *There used to be a time when you could just say a rhyme*
> *and*

> *Wouldn't have to worry about one of your people dyin'*
> *But now it's elevated, 'cause once*
> *you put someone's kids in it*
> *The shit gets escalated — it ain't just words no more,*
>   *is it?*

Another incident that may have soured Eminem on beefing was Fifty Cent being stabbed by one of Ja Rule's cruel in 2000, which Eminem also goes into on the 2004 song *Like Toy Soldiers*.

After Ja's disrespectful public verbal bashing of 50, where he bragged about one of his crew stabbing 50 cent, Eminem gave 50 his blessing to retaliate musically, and thus the beef between 50 and Ja reignited. But here in 2004, Eminem was attempting to shut it down.

> *But I ain't tryna have none of my people hurt or*
>   *murdered*
> *It ain't worth it, I can't think of a perfecter way to*
>   *word it*
> *Than to just say that I love y'all too much to see the*
>   *verdict*
> *I'll walk away from it all 'fore I let it go*
> *any further*

Eminem did walk away from it all. *Like Toy Soldiers* was on his 2005 Encore album and Eminem did not release another main studio album until 2009 Relapse (apart from a Greatest Hits album in 2005.) This was largely because of his drug problem, but who's to say how much the death threats added to the stress that led to the drug problem?

An additional reason for his hiatus was little Hailie's 2004 habit of piling boxes in front of the front door, whenever she knew her dad was supposed to catch a plane to go on tour. Eminem admitted in interviews that this wasn't just lyrics in the song *When I'm Gone*. Hailie really had started to do that, and Marshall needed more time to spend with his children.

The threats to his daughter may have also led to his largely retiring from beefing with other hip-hop artists after 2005. Until Kamikaze.

Kamikaze Beefs

Aside from the major disses to Joe Budden, Tyler, The Creator and Earl Sweatshirt of Odd Future, and Donald Trump already mentioned, several other people were dissed on *Kamikaze*.

The theme of the surprise 2018 album was to hit back at the many people who had been criticizing him in the press, ever since the BET cypher 2017 *The Storm* and his 2017 album *Revival*.

Lord Jamar, a member of a group called *Brand Nubian*, a group that formed in 1989 and has only produced six albums. Lord Jamar spends most of his time doing interviews to comment on social issues. He is a frequent guest on *VladTV*, where he called Eminem "the symbol of white privilege in hip-hop." Lord Jamar has been criticizing Eminem for several years. Claiming Eminem is "only a guest of the culture," Benzino backed Jamar on this claim calling him a cracker and "The White Kid."

The term "culture" has been popularized by the current rap scene and refers to what a rapper is doing or has done for the culture of hip-hop in general. Benzino and Jamar both made the racist claim to the media that Eminem can never be part of the culture as a white man.

This led to Eminem, including a quick diss to Lord Jamar on *Kamikaze*. Marshall compared himself to Elvis Presley as he has done in the past because Elvis was also accused of appropriating black music. He then goes on to emphasize his massive impact on hip-hop culture listing artists clearly inspired by him.

> *And far as Lord Jamar, you better leave me the hell alone*
> *Or I'll show you an Elvis clone*
> *Walk up in this house you own, thrust my pelvic bone*
> *Use your telephone and go fetch me the remote*
> *Put my feet up and just make myself at home*
> *I belong here, clown! Don't tell me 'bout the culture*
> *I inspired the Hopsins, the Logics, the Coles, the Seans, the K-Dots, the 5'9"s, and oh*
> *Brought the world 50 Cent, you did squat, piss and moan*
> *But I'm not gonna fall... bitch! (Yeah)*

Lord Jamar then doubled down on his racial comments by attacking Eminem's use of the word "fetch," claiming it's what slaver owners said to their slaves.

YouTuber *Stiff Kun Recaps* pointed out that Lord Jamar had previously said that he couldn't even understand Eminem when he rapped, claiming he just heard a bunch of gibberish, and random, meaningless rhymes.

But now Jamar was suddenly accusing Eminem of including subtle dog-whistle racism in his suddenly coherent lyrics. *Stiff Kun Recaps* asked, "Is he (Eminem) deep or not? You've got to pick a fucking narrative."

Also, it's pretty clear that Eminem was saying he was going to make himself at home in Jamar's house (referring to how Jamar said he was only a guest in the house of hip-hop) and that he was going to fetch *himself* the remote. He was not ordering Jamar to get the remote.

Stiff Kun Recaps, a black YouTuber and big hip-hop fan, goes onto say how much he hates Lord Jamar's racism.

DJ Akademiks was another target for Eminem, on the song *Fall.* DJ Akademiks, real name Livingston Allen, hosted a YouTube channel called *Everyday Struggle* with Joe Budden, which is reported to make one million dollars annually with his YouTube channel.

Allen was quick to dismiss Revival as "trash" when it released.

Akademiks also made fun of Eminem on his channel, when a video of Marshall and a younger woman in a hotel room surfaced online. This turned out to be only a promotional video for the *River* music video, and promotion for Eminem's 2017 *Revival* album, but Akademiks had laughed at Eminem for getting caught out with a "thot" an acronym for "that hoe over there" which has become a contemporary slang term for a woman who shows off her body a lot, and is in some way common rather than sophisticated.

Ultimately Akademiks only made a fool of himself here as the stunt with Eminem and the young woman was only promotion for the *Revival* album.

Eminem flips this misconception into a witty double entendre, claiming that he would never be caught with a thot (which is a homophone of thought) even while "getting brain" (receiving fellatio).

Back to Akademiks

Say this shit is trash again, I'll have you twisted

> *Like you had it when you thought you had me slippin'*
>   *at the telly*
> *Even when I'm gettin' brain, you'll never catch me*
>   *with a thot*

Charlamagne Tha God, was another target, on both the songs *Fall* and *The Ringer*.

Lenard McKelvey (Charlamagne) is an American radio DJ and television personality, who likes to refer to himself as "the Hip Hop Howard Stern." A name more often given to Joe Budden by the press.

Charlamagne Tha God & Joe Budden had a segment on Revolt TV, presenting the Dope/Trash artists of the year. On their 2017 show, Charlamagne said that Eminem had to go on the trash list for the year.

McKelvey claimed that Eminem's 2017 BET Hip-Hop Awards, dismissing Donald Trump, had "subpar bars," and criticized his wordplay referring to a comic book character.

> *Racism's the only thing he's fantastic for*
> *'Cause that's how he gets his fuckin' rocks off, and*
>   *he's orange*
> *Yeah, sick tan*
> *That's why he wants us to disband*
> *'Cause he cannot withstand*
> *The fact we're not afraid of Trump*
> *Fuck walkin' on eggshells, I came to stomp*
> *That's why he keeps screamin', "Drain the swamp!"*
> *'Cause he's in quicksand*

Eminem here compares Trump to a comic book character from the Fantastic Four created by Stan Lee. The monstrous "Thing" is a man named Ben Grimm, a character who develops superpowers after exposure to cosmic rays. The Thing is a massive creature with tremendous durability and strength due to the nature of his rock-like flesh

Marshall compared the Thing's orange color to Trump's fake tan and makes a play on words about Trump getting his "rocks" off from racism.

Charlamagne claimed he liked the antiracism message of *The Storm* but hated the lyrics. He claimed to be a comic book fan himself and said it was a reach because he claimed the Thing wasn't orange, he was yellow or beige, and that he had nothing to do with rocks.

Eminem responded on Kamikaze in is song *The Ringer*.

> *"Aw, man! That BET cypher was weak, it was garbage*
> *The Thing ain't even orange—oh my God, that's a reach!"*
> *Shout to all my colorblind people*
> *Each and every one of y'all, if you call a fire engine green*
> *Aquamarine or you think water is pink*
> *"Dawg, that's a date." "Looks like an olive to me."*
> *"Look, there's an apple!" No, it's not,*
> *it's a peach!*

On *The Breakfast Club,* Charlamagne admitted that these bars on Kamikaze were" slick." He seemed impressed at the way Eminem was quoting him verbatim and rhyming as well. Also interesting was the fact Eminem's mother frequently refers to herself as color blind, though not literally. When Debbie Mathers refers to herself as color blind, she tends to mean she's not at all racist.

Later in *The Ringer,* Eminem spits

> *Charlamagne gonna hate anyway, doesn't matter what*
> *I say*
> *Give me Donkey of the Day*

This is in reference to Charlamagne's popular syndicated weekday morning show *The Breakfast Club* on *New York's Power 105.1*. On this show, he has a "Donkey of the Day," being someone he called out for foolishness.

Charlamagne admitted, however, that he thought Kamikaze was a "dope album."

Eminem also references Charlamagne in the song *The Fall*.

> *One last time for Charlamagne*
> *If my response is late, it's just how long it takes*
> *To hit my fuckin' radar, I'm so far away*

Here Eminem apologizes for the delayed response to all his critics, implying that he's so far above the criticism or so wealthy, successful, or busy working that it takes a long time to hit his radar.

In his career, Eminem has mostly stayed away from the bragging and flexing so common among other rappers. One notable exception being the song *Rap God*. However, after the smackdown people gave him over *Revival*; however, Eminem starts bragging about his skill and even his wealth in post *Revival* songs such as *Kill Shot* and *Greatest*. He even pokes a little fun at his very famous co-stars, Drake, Lil Wayne, and Kayne West on the song *Forever*, Eminem spits,

> *The fans waited for this moment like that feature*
> *When I stole the show (Ha), sorry if I took forever*
>   *(Ha-ha)*

Fans quickly claimed he was dissing Drake on the
   song *Kamikaze,* in lines such as
Put me on a track, I go cray on it like a color book
You got some views, but you're still below me
Mine are higher, so when you compare our views, you
   get overlooked
And I don't say the hook unless I wrote the hook

Fans were sure Marshall included the word "views" because of Drake's 2016 album views and because of media stories about Drake using ghostwriters. However, Eminem's lawyer and manager Paul Rosenberg didn't like this. On Twitter, Paul said, "He isn't dissing Drake. Dead that." In the Sway interview, Eminem said, "I'll always be grateful for something Drake did for one of my daughters."

Eminem names a few new young rappers, but he's not really starting a beef, he just says he doesn't dig them, because they aren't lyrically good.

Get this fuckin' audio out my Audi, yo, adiós
I can see why people like Lil Yachty, but not me
   though
Not even dissin', it just ain't for me
All I am simply is just an emcee
Maybe "Stan" just isn't your cup of tea (Get it?)
Maybe your cup's full of syrup and lean

Marshall goes relatively easy on these young rappers he has no personal beefs with, even those who are famous for being lyrically horrendous like Lil Pump, making fun of their nonsense rhymes he says only,

So, finger-bang, chicken wang, MGK, Igg' Azae.'

Lil Pump, Lil Xan imitate Lil Wayne
I should aim at everybody in the game
Pick a name
I'm fed up with bein' humble
And rumor is I'm hungry, I'm sure you heard rumblings
I heard you wanna rumble like an empty stomach
I heard your mumblin', but it's jumbled in mumbo-jumbo
The era that I'm from will pummel
you, that's what it's comin' to
What the fuck you gonna do

As well as his political diss to Donald Trump on *Kamikaze* about him being a serpent that sold a dream that he's deserted, Eminem also goes at Mike Pence on the album, on the song The Ringer.

While I take my ball sack and flick it like a light switch
Like Vice President Mike Pence
Back up on my shit in a sidekick as I lay it on a spike strip
These are things that I'd rather do than hear you on a mic

Eminem refers to Mike Pence's former claims that government money provided to AIDS charities would be better spent on the prevention of homosexuality, through institutions that claim they can prevent it. This was presumed by many to mean through electric shock therapy. Here Eminem invokes imagery of shock therapy on his testicles, among other torturous things that could be done to one's genitals all as another diss to rappers like Lil Yachty. (who is mentioned earlier on this track.) Eminem jokes that he'd rather have torture on his genitals than listen to that kind of rap since nine-tenths of it is about jewelry.

Machine Gun Kelly

While Machine Gun Kelly tried to pretend that Eminem dissed him on *Not Alike* over his 2012 tweet about Hailie, Eminem had, in fact, been hearing from friends over several weeks that Kelly had dissed him on a March 2, 2018, Tech N9ne song *No Reason*. It was a subliminal diss.

> *"It's only one option, you gon' need a doctor/I ain't talkin' 'bout the one from Compton/I pop cherries and popstars, you popsicles is not hard/Popped in on the top charts out the cop car/To remind y'all you just rap and not God and I don't care who got bars,"*

After checking out Kelly's twitter and seeing more disses, Marshall realized it was time to answer MGK back, especially since the concept of his 2018 album *Kamikaze* was to finally answer back to all the people who'd been dissing him.

Eminem struck back on the 2018 track *Not Alike*.

> *"This little cock-sucker, he must be feeling himself*
> *He wants to keep up his tough demeanor*
> *So, he does a feature, decides to team up with Nina*
> *But next time you don't gotta use Tech N9ne*
> *If you wanna come at me with a sub, Machine Gun*

> *And I'm talking to you, but you already know who the fuck you are, Kelly."*

Eminem cleverly connects MGK to the disgraced R. Kelly by saying "are Kelly," among other witticisms.

Eminem said it a year and a half after MGK tweeted that he started to go down the rabbit hole of YouTube videos and was disgusted to find MGK doing a press run to talk about his daughter.

Marshall then watched in disbelief as YouTube video after video revealed MGK talking to the media about how he had tweeted that sixteen-year-old Hailie was "hot as fuck." Eminem said, "I'm like, "what the *fuck*? Yo, my man better chill."

Eminem said this was not, however, the reason he dissed Machine Gun Kelly on his 2018 *Kamikaz*e album because he didn't even know about it at the time. The reason was MGK's other disses in songs such as his *LA Leakers Freestyle* Kelly rapped

> *"I'm my favorite rapper alive*
> *Since my favorite rapper banned me from*
> *Shade 45."*

Eminem's response to this in his Sway interview was savage. "Like I'm trying to hinder his career. I don't give a fuck about your career. Do you think I actually fucking think about you? Do you know how many rappers there are out there that are better than you? You're not even in the conversation.

But then when you get on Tech N9ne's album and start sending shots, and people keep hitting me up saying Yo Kelly dissed you, he dissed you, and this was on the heels of the freestyle he did mentioning *Shade 45* (I'm thinking) shut the fuck up! Shut the fuck up!"

MGK had also tweeted, "You just rap you're not God," a reference to Eminem's 2013 song *Rap God*.

MGK also decided to answer Eminem's brief 2018 diss on Not Alike with a full diss track called *Rap Devil*.

Eminem denies doing anything to hamper MGK's career. It seems from what Sway himself said though that one of Eminem's people may have seen the tweet and banned MGK from Shade 45 without Eminem knowing a thing about it.

Sway said he invited Kelly to come for an interview on the station but then got word from other staff to uninvite him two years before the news about the tweet even hit Marshall's radar.

Rap Devil was the most Googled search phrase of the first two weeks of September 2018. Producer Ronald Oneil Spence, Jr., professionally known as Ronny J, made a great beat for the song, getting the song a lot of attention.

Other rappers have made full diss tracks on Eminem that didn't get noticed at all, but MGK was backed by Bad Boy Records and Interscope and had a music video. The song's title was, of course, a play on Eminem's 2013 track *Rap God*.

Rap Devil peaked at number 13 on the *Billboard Hot 100* singles chart in the United States. *Rap Devil* also generated over 13.9 million views on YouTube during its first 24 hours, landing it in the number one spot for YouTube trending for multiple days. It currently sits in the top fifteen hundred most viewed songs of all time on YouTube.

Eminem went on to tell radio personality and rapper, Sway Calloway,

"Now I'm in this fuckin' weird thing, because I'm like, 'I gotta answer this motherfucker.' And every time I do that, it makes that person -- as irrelevant as people say I am in hip-hop -- I make them bigger by getting into this thing, where I'm like, 'I want to destroy him.' But I also don't want to make him bigger," Eminem explains. "Because now you're a fucking enemy. I'll leave it at that. I'm not sure exactly what I'm going to do at this point right now."

Eventually, he answered Kelly with the phenomenally successful track *Killshot*. The Machine Gun Kelly diss is the third-highest music video debut overall ever. *Killshot* debuted at number three on the US Billboard Hot 100 in its first week.

Killshot, which came out on Sept. 14, 2018, stormed out of the gate with a massive 38.1 million views in its first 24 hours. The only two music videos ever to top that debut figure are Taylor Swift, whose *Look What You Made Me Do* earned 43.2 million views in August 2017 and BTS, whose music video for the song *Idol* set the all-time YouTube debut record with 45 million views in August 2018.

The song holds the record for the number one most viewed audio-only release on the YouTube platform. It is also the biggest YouTube debut for a hip-hop video ever, surpassing Kanye West's and Lil Pump's *I Love It*.

Killshot was viewed so many times in its first 24 hours on YouTube that the counter broke, and for a while, the ability to post comments glitched and broke.

It is the twelfth most viewed video in its first twenty-four hours in all of YouTube's history. *Killshot* broke the Genius record for being the fastest song to hit a million page views, hitting a million in just 8 hours. Killshot became eligible for Platinum despite being only a single diss track with no video.

People have begged Eminem to perform *Killshot* in concert, but Marshall refuses. Probably because he doesn't want to make MGK bigger.

MGK has a reported estimated net worth of eight million, so it's funny he should complain

Oscar, the Grouch, chill on the couch (Fuck)
You got an Oscar, damn
Can anyone else get some food in their mouth? (For real)
Eminem plays along with this game in *Killshot* regardless
Luxury, oh, you broke, bitch?
Yeah, I had enough money in '02
To burn it in front of you, ho

Admittedly a guy with a net worth of eight million might feel like a "broke bitch" compared to a guy with a net worth of two hundred and ten million and rapidly climbing.

CHAPTER TEN

I still live like I budget at Gilbert's Lodge
Check stub, bizzle
So, fuck Sizzler!
These checkers are bust like a blood blister

Random Facts
(Know your facts before you come at me, lil' goof.)

- EMINEM ONCE TWEETED THAT WATCHING THE MOVIE *THE Truman Show* influenced the lyrics of *The Eminem Show* a lot. This was because, by 2002, he felt like he was living in a goldfish bowl with all the public attention.

- As a child, Marshall loved comic books of many kinds and dreamed of being a comic book artist. He teased his mother about *Casper, the Friendly Ghost* living in their house, and kept telling her not to sit on Casper and that Casper had walked through walls.

By the time the 1995 *Casper* movie came out (based on

the Harvey Comics cartoon character), Kim was pregnant. Kim's pregnancy renewed Marshall's interest in all things to do with childhood, and he went to see the movie.

During the movie, he was impressed with the performance of Devon Sawa, who played Casper in human form. This led to Eminem later contacting Devon to play Stan in his music video.

- Marshall got evicted the night before the 1997 Rap Olympics and had to break into his own place and sleep on the floor before leaving for LA.

-Eminem collectively sold more than 32.2 million albums during the 2000s, making him the best-selling artist of the decade.

-Marshall is the third bestselling artist of the 2010s after Adele and Taylor Swift.

-*D12* is called *D12* short for dirty dozen. They were six members, each with a dual personality. The creation of each of their alternative personalities was the inspiration for Eminem's alter ego Slim Shady.

-Eminem announced the end of *D12* as a group on the song Stepping Stones featured on his 2019 album Kamikaze. He explains that "it's not goodbye to the friendship but *D12* is over."

In the song, Marshall also explains he has found it too hard to shoulder the expectations that he can help every one of his friends' solo careers.

-Eminem is left-handed, a trait widely associated with creativity.

-Marshall is five-foot-seven inches tall. (Shorter than Kim, who is five foot eleven.)

-*Rolling Stone* ranked him as the 82nd greatest artist of all time.

- Despite his bad-boy image, the only time Eminem had

ever been arrested before his concealed weapons charges was at age twenty. He and his friends had driven by some people and shot at one of them with a paintball gun. But while Eminem showed up in court, the victim did not show up, and so the case was dropped.

-*Infinite* was released in 1996 it sold less than 500 copies.

-Runyon Avenue is a street that runs off 8 Mile Road in Detroit. All of the members from D12, including Eminem, hail from renting on Runyon Ave.

- In 2014 Eminem's publishers sued the right-wing New Zealand National Party after The National Party used a piece of music remarkably similar to the song *Lose Yourself* in one of its election ads.

Eminem's lawyers said the music used by National, together with the theme of the advertisement, was clearly an attempt to invoke the spirit of *Lose Yourself* without permission. Permission that would never have been granted under any circumstances.

The song *Lose Yourself* charts the struggle of a rapper to overcome his nerves before eventual success.

Eminem's publisher's lawyer Joel Martin said "They licensed this from a company who ... offered it as *Emin-eske*, and they (the National Party) were looking for something very specifically like *Lose Yourself*," It's kind of like saying I bought a Gucci handbag off the street and somebody told me it was a Gucci and it kind of looks like a Gucci and it feels like a Gucci, but it only cost me $10. Well, if you know that Gucci bags cost a thousand dollars, you would suspect that there would be something wrong."

Joel Martin said the National Party ad "picked up on the theme of the song "if you had one shot, one opportunity...in this case, the choice is clear. That they attempted to do that so blatantly and say that it wasn't *Lose Yourself* is just absurd," the lawyer said.

The comedian John Oliver made fun of the *New Zealand National Party* buying a track called *Emin-eske*, saying they should have chosen a less obviously stolen title like *"This May or May not be Copyright Infringement,"* or *"Please Don't Tell Anyone About This."*

8 Mile Style won the case.

-Eminem, at age forty-six years old, was 2018's highest-selling artist worldwide.

He outsold every artist across the globe – with a huge 755,027 album sales bagged, far ahead of second-place finishers BTS, according to BuzzAngle Music's 2018 Year-End Report.

Eminem's tenth studio album *Kamikaze* was only the tenth bestselling album of the year; however, the findings show that it was Marshal Mathers' extensive back catalog that catapulted him to the top. He outsold The Beatles, Queen, and Taylor Swift for the year.

CHAPTER ELEVEN

But you keep treatin' me like a staircase: it's time to fuckin' step
And I won't be comin' back, so don't hold your fuckin' breath

---

When will Eminem Retire?
(Full of controversy until I retire my jersey.)

IN 2019 EMINEM WAS STILL DOING SOME OF HIS TRADEMARK offending people. Janice Dickinson slammed Eminem as a "little prick" when interviewed by the *Daily Mail*. "I was fucking offended," Dickenson said.

This happened because of Boogie and Eminem's 2019 song *Rainy Days* which included the lines

But when you got nothing to say except for the hand your

dick is in
And if your plan's to stick it in Janice Dickinson
Imagine if the Temazepam is kickin' in,
It's havin' you i8panic-stricken

"When I first heard those lyrics, I was taken aback," Dickenson said. "It's referring to the recent Bill Cosby sexual abuse trial, that I went to for Andrea Constand back in Philadelphia and that I too was raped without consent back in 1982 by Bill Cosby and all of those things came into my head."

Eventually, however, Dickenson was convinced by friends to accept that being mentioned in an Eminem song in any way is an honor.

"It's not nice to be dropped into a song in this context, but it's phenomenal to be associated with Eminem in any way possible. Don't get me wrong, I'm a diehard Eminem number one fan, he's a god, and he writes legendary songs… But when I heard the lyrics, I didn't know how to think or feel."

Another recent scandal occurred because Eminem dropped the line, "Bitch, I'm off the chain like Kala Brown."

The line is a reference to the South Carolina woman who was found chained in a storage container on the property of serial killer Todd Kohlhepp. Brown was kidnapped and spent over two months "chained like a dog" in a metal container on the serial killer's property.

Several people expressed outrage at the line, but in a

statement through her spokesperson, Brown addressed the unexpected reference.

"We have seen all of the attention regarding Eminem referencing Kala in one of his newly released songs," the spokesperson said.

"At this time, given we fully know and understand Eminem's style of rap music (it can come off a little unnerving) but she does not want to take offense or feel as if he is attacking her personally. It was a clever line that rhymed, and we'd like to leave it at that. Everyone expresses themselves in their own way, and if anything, people will always feel a flash of Kala's struggle when hearing that line."

These were two 2019 examples of Eminem carrying on the tradition of "If your name rhymes with something… good." It's a mistake to think every rhyme and mention is an intended diss.

Calls for Eminem to retire, to "put down the mic, or put down the pen" have been frequent from his haters.

Some of these people love to harp on about the fact he's over forty. Often these public attacks are ploys by "haters" to get money for themselves through mentioning his name in a negative way.

Examples of such "haters," include other rappers, various journalists, and also YouTubers. The YouTube channel, *King Trending*, has frequently made videos with clickbait titles, claiming Eminem is quitting that have no basis in fact.

As promotion for *The Marshall Mathers LP2*, Eminem attended an event on *Facebook,* where fans were able to ask him questions for five minutes. One of the last questions asked was, "What pisses you off most?" Eminem's response was "when people ask me if I'm retiring."

Admittedly, however, Eminem has lyrically played with

the idea of retiring, in many songs, in order to taunt haters and fans alike.

Even as far back as 1999 in his official dance track from *The Slim Shady LP*, *Cum on Everybody* Eminem raps:

Fuck rap, I'm givin' it up, y'all, I'm sorry
(But Eminem, this is your record release party)

Genius.com annotation on this song states that Eminem making empty threats to quit rap is a "long-running joke," funny here because he's threatening to quit even before his first major release.

In 2002, in the song, *Say Goodbye Hollywood*, Eminem reflects on the fact he might have had to say goodbye to his fame and success after being arrested for possession of a concealed weapon and for assault.

In 2004 the song, *When I'm Gone,* played with ideas around quitting rap, quitting drugs and death, and also heralded his very real temporary retirement to get clean and spend more time with his kids.

Other songs that have flirted with the idea of quitting have always turned out to just be expressions of his frustrations with his career in the moment and nothing more profound.

In 2007 Eminem had planned a comeback album which he planned to call, *King Mathers,* the scrapped album contained an "outro," song *It's Been Real*, including the lyrics

Thanks, it's been real
I love you, but I just can't deal
With the stress, this game is giving me...

The rest of the lyrics read like the acknowledgments in a book a simple thank you to various people in his life and a goodbye.

The song *It's Been Real* was written immediately after Proof death, and so is believed to be a real goodbye song.

Some people claim that this was meant to be his last song released ever and a real goodbye and planned retirement, but *King Mathers* seems more likely to have been a comeback attempt, one that Marshall ultimate decided just didn't make the grade.

Eminem never officially released *It's Been Real;* the song was eventually leaked against his wishes.

Much of *King Mathers* was written while Eminem was in his worst place on drugs before his serious overdose in December 2007. In the leaked song from the album G.O.A.T, Eminem makes a reference to the general public believing that he's done with rap.

Everyone thinks that my career is down the tubes
And I'm in some dusty garage
Inhalin' them carbon monoxide fumes

Beautiful was the only King Mathers song that Marshall didn't junk. Included on his *Relapse* album, Eminem made yet another threat to quit rap forever.

But I just can't admit
Or come to grips, with the fact that
I may be done with rap, I need a new outlet

MTV's 2007 and 2009 lists of *the 10 Hottest MCs in the Game* left Eminem out completely. The 2009 exclusion was particularly painful, considering Relapse was the bestselling album of 2009.

In 2010 in the song *25 To Life*.
Eminem responds to this with

But when you spoke of people
Who meant the most to you, you left me off your list?
Fuck you, hip hop! I'm leavin' you
My life sentence is served, bitch

On the album *Revival*, Eminem stirred fans anxieties again with lines like:

I'll put out this last album then I'm done with it
One-hundred percent finished
Fed up with it,
I'm hanging it up, fuck it!

Lines repeated in both *Castle* and at the very end of the album in the song *Arose*.

But those songs were both about his drug overdoes of 2007 and the album was quickly followed by the 2018 album *Kamikaze*.

Very shortly after *Kamikaze's* release Eminem gave fans a treat with the Machine Gun Kelly diss track *Killshot*, on which he gave fans reason to believe he would never willingly retire.

It's funny but so true
I'd rather be 80-year-old me than 20-year-old you
'Til I'm hitting old age
Still can fill a whole page with a 10-year-old's rage

In the 2019 Ed Sheeran hit *Remember the Name* featuring Eminem and 50 Cent, Eminem doubles down on this concept.

Not even when I'm on my deathbed
Man, I feel like Ed, it isn't time to drop the mic yet
So why would I quit?
The thought that I would stop when I'm dead
Just popped in my head

The reference to "feeling like Ed," appears to be agreeing with Sheeran's assertions that despite all his riches he still wants way more, and has no intention of quitting.

The lyric Eminem raps about performing even on his deathbed might possibly be an allusion to David Bowie, who performed the music video for his song 2015 *Lazarus* after being told his cancer was terminal and that his doctors were ending his treatment. Bowie died of liver cancer only three days after the release of the *Lazarus* music video and two days after the release of *Blackstar* in January 2016.

Songs such as *Killshot* and *Remember the Name* show Eminem has no intention of being bullied out of the game or accepting ageist assessments of his ability to continue to rap.

Marshall's hero Ice T is still rapping and making music videos at sixty. In August 2019, Ice T released the track *Too Old for The Dumb Shit*. Eminem, in his late forties, looks set for a bright future where he continues to give fans plenty of content.

In the Anderson Cooper interview of 2010, Eminem spoke about being bullied, and about his song *Not Afraid*, saying. "I think the message (of the song) will resonate with many kids contemplating an easy way out. Even the biggest of stars have gone through bullying and survived it and, furthermore, have come out on top... so can you.

Did you enjoy reading *Not Afraid: Secrets of Eminem*? Then please recommend it to a friend! ☺
Leaving reviews also helps authors out.

Cover photo belongs to Wikimedia Commons.

CONNECT WITH LISA

Website: https://lisawhitefern.wordpress.com
Facebook: https://business.facebook.com/LisaWhitefernRomance/
Twitter: https://twitter.com/LisaWhitefern

Sign up for Lisa and WatermarkNZ Press Newsletter: http://eepurl.com/dvi2In

CPSIA information can be obtained
at www.ICGtesting.com
Printed in the USA
LVHW050745050722
722721LV00014B/116